MY POCKET

MEDITATIONS

~FOR~

SELF-COMPASSION

ANYTIME EXERCISES FOR SELF-ACCEPTANCE,
KINDNESS, AND PEACE

COURTNEY E. ACKERMAN

ADAMS MEDIA

NEW YORK   LONDON   TORONTO   SYDNEY   NEW DELHI

Aadamsmedia

Adams Media
An Imprint of Simon & Schuster, Inc.
57 Littlefield Street
Avon, Massachusetts 02322

First Adams Media trade paperback
edition June 2020

ADAMS MEDIA and colophon are
trademarks of Simon & Schuster.

For information about special
discounts for bulk purchases,
please contact Simon & Schuster
Special Sales at 1-866-506-1949
or business@simonandschuster.com.

The Simon & Schuster Speakers
Bureau can bring authors to your
live event. For more information or
to book an event contact the Simon
& Schuster Speakers Bureau at
1-866-248-3049 or visit our website
at www.simonspeakers.com.

Interior design by Julia Jacintho
Interior images © 123RF/Ekaterina
Matveeva

Manufactured in China

10 9 8 7 6 5 4 3 2

Library of Congress Cataloging-in-
Publication Data
Names: Ackerman, Courtney E., author.
Title: My pocket meditations for self-
compassion / Courtney E. Ackerman.
Description: Avon, Massachusetts:
Adams Media, 2020.
Series: My pocket.
Includes index.
Identifiers: LCCN 2019055334 |
ISBN 9781507213490 (pb) |
ISBN 9781507213506 (ebook)
Subjects: LCSH: Self-acceptance. |
Compassion. | Meditation.
Classification: LCC BF575.S37 A25
2020 | DDC 158.1/28--dc23
LC record available at
https://lccn.loc.gov/2019055334

ISBN 978-1-5072-1349-0
ISBN 978-1-5072-1350-6 (ebook)

CONTENTS

INTRODUCTION

Are you looking for a way to become more accepting of yourself? Do you want to get more in tune with your authentic inner self? Are you searching for ideas to boost your self-love?

If so, you need to practice self-compassion.

Why is self-compassion so important? Because it encourages you to go easier on yourself, which in turn makes it easier to love yourself and cope with all of life's challenges. When you have self-compassion, you are better able to understand your emotions, give and receive love, let go of past mistakes, and move forward with confidence. It can often be tempting to leave this validation and compassion up to others, but it's vital that you learn to do this for yourself. And if you want other people to be kinder and more understanding toward you, you need to set a precedent by being kind and understanding toward yourself first. To put it simply, your well-being rests on the foundation of how you think about yourself.

If you want to work on building up that inner foundation, *My Pocket Meditations for Self-Compassion* can help. Inside you'll find 150 ways to express kindness and compassion toward yourself, make peace with your emotions, build your resiliency, and learn not only to accept but also to appreciate exactly who you are. Meditation is the key to helping foster this growth because it enhances the areas of the brain that are responsible for empathy, creativity, and compassion— all necessary factors in self-acceptance.

You can pick a chapter at random or go through in a purposeful order; it's all up to you. You'll find techniques for developing and strengthening different variations to self-love and self-compassion, including:

* Meditations on Self-Acceptance
* Meditations on Self-Appreciation
* Meditations on Self-Forgiveness
* Meditations on Being Body Positive
* Meditations on Accepting Love

Working on perfecting these techniques will remind you that you are worthy and deserving of love and will fill you with more self-awareness, kindness, and peace!

PREPARING TO MEDITATE

If you've never meditated before, you'll find this guide to be a handy resource to help you build an effective meditation practice. The first question new meditators usually have is something like, "But how am I supposed to clear my mind? I can't just sit and think about nothing!" However, as you'll see, meditating is not just "sitting and thinking about nothing," although it might look like that from the outside. Meditating is a useful addition to anyone's life, but before you start trying out specific meditations, you have to get the basics down.

Before you start meditating, make sure to practice these steps:

1. Find somewhere comfortable to sit or lie down—just make sure it's not so comfortable that you're likely to fall asleep.

2. Close your eyes and bring your awareness to your breath. For a few moments, just follow your breath as it travels through your nose, down your windpipe, and into your lungs, then back out the same way. Notice the natural rhythm of your breath.

3. Now slowly begin to control your breath. Regulate your breathing, taking three seconds to inhale, pausing for a moment, then taking three seconds to exhale, followed by another pause. Fill your lungs all the way, then expel all the air.

4. Once you've got a good handle on your breathing, turn your attention to your thoughts. Detach yourself from your thoughts by noticing them, but refrain from holding on to them. Don't attempt to rigidly control your thoughts, just let them enter your mind and drift back out just as easily.

5. Practice observing your thoughts and letting them go until you have a clear mind—or at least a mostly clear mind.

6. Now you're ready to meditate! Pick an exercise and get to it.

It can seem awkward and unfamiliar the first few times you try to meditate, but with a little practice it will start to feel like second nature.

CHAPTER 1

MEDITATIONS ON SELF-ACCEPTANCE

Self-acceptance is the main building block of self-compassion. It is the foundation upon which you construct your self-love and a jumping-off point for feeling compassion for yourself. Without self-acceptance, you do not have a good basis for understanding and appreciating yourself. Before you get into the techniques, there's an important point to be made about self-acceptance: It doesn't mean you give yourself a free pass on any bad behavior or excuse every mistake you have made in the past. Self-acceptance means only that you accept all of it, the good and the bad, as a part of yourself. The meditations in this chapter will help you do just that—instead of denying, avoiding, or making excuses for yourself, these meditations will teach you how to accept yourself as the imperfect but ultimately good person that you are.

PRACTICE SITTING WITH YOURSELF

It might not feel natural at first, but learning to sit with yourself is one of the most beneficial things you can do. In today's busy, non-stop world, it's common to fill even the smallest of spaces with entertainment. We check our phones on elevators, scroll through social media when there's a single dull moment at work, and watch videos or read blogs at the dinner table. While none of these activities are inherently bad, they can be used as distractions from enjoying and appreciating ourselves.

Instead of letting these small moments go to waste, use them to practice mindfulness and build your capacity for self-compassion. Here's how:

1. After taking the necessary steps to prepare for meditation, bring your awareness to your environment. Think about where you are and what is around you. Put together a good mental picture of your surroundings.

2. Next, bring your awareness to yourself. See yourself with your mind's eye, sitting calmly and peacefully. Be mindful of your current emotional state and what you are doing. Try to accept yourself as you are, right now, in this moment.

3. Stay here for a minute or two, just enjoying sitting with yourself. If it helps, give yourself a little pat on the back for making time for meditation.

MEDITATE ON
YOUR PAST SELF

Although we are generally the same people as we were yesterday, many of us feel like very different people than we were thirty, twenty, or even ten years ago. We all go through major changes in our lives, some of which can be transformational.

If you've never taken the time to reflect on this growth, this exercise is a perfect opportunity to give it a try!

1. Grab a journal and a pen, then prepare to meditate.
2. Pick a time to focus on. You can write down "age twenty-five" or "at my first job" or even get specific with the date, like "September 2004."
3. Close your eyes and spend a few minutes focusing on yourself at this point in time. Think about what was going on in your life then, what you valued, who was important to you, what was stressing you out or weighing on you, and what your goals and dreams were.
4. Write down all the details that come to mind. Try to paint an accurate picture of who you were at that point in your life.
5. Draw the timeline between then and now, either in your head or on paper. Think about all that has happened between now and then, and see how far you've come.

Reflecting on your past self is a great way to cultivate compassion and respect for yourself and all the hard work you've put into your career, your relationships, and your self-development.

MEDITATE ON
YOUR PRESENT SELF

Becoming more compassionate for yourself requires knowing and accepting who you are. To become more familiar with who you are, practice a meditation focused on getting to know and feeling comfortable with your present self.

To cultivate better self-knowledge and self-acceptance, follow these steps:

1. Once you're prepared to meditate, sit quietly for a few moments and focus on regular breathing. Try to clear your mind of any "junk" that might be weighing you down. Let your thoughts come and go, but don't hang on to any of them.

2. Shift your focus from a clear mind to your present self. See yourself in your mind's eye, and take in this view for a moment.

3. Think about the person you are today, and place this current self in context with all the experiences that have brought you here. For example, are you a kind person? What has influenced you toward being a kind person?

4. Think of your key traits and characteristics. What makes you the person you are? Is it your job, your skills and talents, your relationships, your approach to life, your hobbies? What words do you use to define yourself?

5. Spend a few minutes getting to know yourself. Store some of this in your mind's "self-knowledge" folder so you can pull from it later to give yourself some informed self-acceptance.

MEDITATE ON
YOUR FUTURE SELF

If you're the type of person who rarely looks to the future, you might be surprised at how much self-knowledge and self-acceptance you have to gain from looking forward. If you *are* the sort of person to consider your future, this exercise can help you by making the process a little more structured and combining it with meditation that's focused on self-acceptance.

Follow these steps to give this meditation a try:

1. Grab a journal or notebook to write in and prepare to meditate as you usually do.
2. Keep your eyes closed and think about a certain point in your future. It can be a month ahead, a year ahead, or twenty years ahead—the distance doesn't really matter, but you should pick a time that you feel will be significant (e.g., when you're working at your dream job, retiring, or sending your kids off to college). Make a note of this future point in time in your journal.
3. Think about who you will be. How do you think you will have changed? For example, will you be a skilled and regular meditator at that time? Will you have mastered the skill you want to learn at work? Write down the specifics you foresee.
4. Send some acceptance and appreciation to your future self. Remind yourself that you *will be* that person far off in the distance one day, and give that person a mental hug.

ACCEPT
THE REALITY

Humans are remarkably good at changing the narrative, and it's often a subconscious process. When we don't like the way something is going in our lives, we might simply reframe it, think about it in different terms, and make ourselves feel a little bit better about it. This can be beneficial when you reframe the things you can't change to better cope with hardship, but it can also distract you from dealing with things in a healthy manner. To get to know and accept yourself better, consider this practice of accepting your reality.

1. Once you're prepared and ready to meditate, turn your attention toward yourself, but with a third-party perspective. Look at yourself as if you are looking at another person.

2. "Zoom out" on your life, seeing the big picture. Think about yourself in the broader context of your life: where you are, what you're doing on a daily basis, who you interact with regularly, and so on.

3. Note whether there is anything in your life that is unsatisfactory or isn't going quite the way you want it to. Don't go looking for the negative, but open yourself up to a nonjudgmental observation of what is.

4. Now, try to accept your reality. Accept all the parts of your life, both good and bad. Make peace with the fact that there may be some ways in which your life is not ideal, and that's okay.

TAKE A GOOD, HARD LOOK
AT YOURSELF

While it can be tough to see your own flaws, self-examination is critical to accepting yourself and feeling a healthy sense of compassion and love for yourself. They say you can't love someone unless you know them—*really* know them—and the same is true of loving yourself. It's a much healthier and more satisfying self-love when you are truly accepting yourself as you are, and to do that you need to know who you are.

Here's how to take a good, hard look at yourself:

1. When you're ready, focus your attention on yourself. Take a third-person view, seeing yourself as if you're looking at someone else. It can help to literally visualize yourself as you are right now, sitting quietly and meditating.

2. Think about what makes this person who they are. What are their characteristics, their unique traits, their funny quirks? What are their strengths and weaknesses? What do they wish they could change about themselves?

3. Take note of the main qualities or characteristics that come to mind, including the not-so-desirable ones. Remind yourself that your goal is to be observant and nonjudgmental, not to chastise yourself.

4. Make peace with the fact that this person is you. You come complete with positive qualities, flaws and negative features, and everything in between. Remember that this is what it means to be human.

After nonjudgmentally identifying and accepting your flaws in this exercise, you can work on improving them in a healthy manner.

PRACTICE
RADICAL ACCEPTANCE

"Radical acceptance" is sort of a funny term; the two words simply don't seem to go together! How can you "radically" accept something? Although it might seem like a nonsensical combination, it's actually a powerful technique that you can use to enhance your self-acceptance and, through this, your self-compassion.

Follow these instructions to give it a try:

1. Once you're ready to meditate, take a few more long, cleansing breaths. Extend your inhale to at least four seconds, pause, then stretch your exhale out to at least four seconds, and pause again.

2. Now that you're extra relaxed and centered, bring your awareness to yourself; don't focus on any one thing, like how you look or a strength or a weakness that feels salient right now. Think about yourself in a more abstract way, without homing in on any details.

3. Tell yourself, "I accept you exactly as you are. No thought you have is wrong, no feeling you have is invalid, and nothing you have done is past the reach of your own compassion."

4. Repeat this to yourself as many times as needed to start feeling like it's true.

Radical acceptance is not about absolving you of anything you have done or making you feel like you are beyond reproach; rather, it's about accepting yourself as a flawed human being and creating a foundation to work from. Once you have accepted yourself exactly as you are, you can begin to cultivate real self-respect, self-love, and self-compassion.

FOCUS ON WHO YOU ARE, NOT WHAT YOU DO

If you've ever dabbled in philosophy, especially in the comparison of Eastern and Western philosophy, you might have come into contact with the dichotomy of "being" and "doing." Western cultures tend to focus on "doing," the actions we take and the work we do, while some Eastern cultures tend toward a focus on "being," as in simply existing and being who you are. While there are pros and cons to both ways of thinking, Western cultures are extra prone to the trap of overworking, the need to always be busy, and an irrational fear of being considered lazy. If you find yourself measuring your self-worth in terms of what you do rather than who you are, this meditation can help you find a better balance.

1. Prepare yourself to meditate, then shift your focus from what you are *doing* to who you *are*. Don't think of yourself in terms of what you do, but what you are. For example, reframe your perspective from thinking of yourself in terms of your career or hobbies; instead of thinking, "I'm a software engineer who plays racquetball and fantasy football for fun," think, "I'm a smart and capable person, and I am fun-loving and easygoing."

2. Tell yourself that you are a person who is human and whole, a person who is good enough, and a person who is deserving of love no matter what you do for work or how well you perform.

SET A SELF-ACCEPTANCE INTENTION

Intentions are an excellent tool for making positive changes in your life, and this includes improving your self-acceptance. Intentions are basically decisions that you make on how to conduct yourself and your life going forward; you then put these decisions down into words to give them added weight. They are often found in yoga classes, as instructors will sometimes direct their attendees to set an intention for the class. It might be something like, "Be more mindful of my surroundings," "Listen to what my body is telling me," or simply, "Stay grateful."

You can use this method to help you become more accepting of yourself. Follow these steps to set a self-acceptance intention:

1. After preparing to meditate, give yourself a few more deep, soothing breaths.
2. Next, think about why you want to be more accepting of yourself. Knowing your reasons for setting an intention makes it much easier to stick to it. For example, you might want to be more accepting because you can be overly hard on yourself when you make even a small mistake.
3. With your reasons in mind, set an intention to be more self-accepting. Set it in stone. Do whatever you can to set yourself up for success: Write your intention in your journal, put it on Post-it notes around your house, or set an alarm on your phone to remind you each morning.
4. Commit to carrying your intention out of your meditation session and throughout each day.

FAKE IT 'TIL
YOU FEEL IT

You've undoubtedly heard the old advice, "Fake it 'til you make it!" While this is certainly not a bad recommendation, and many people have succeeded using this philosophy, it's not quite as simple with things like self-acceptance and self-compassion; after all, how do you know when you've "made it"? In light of this, try practicing a slightly different technique: fake it 'til you *feel* it.

This is how you do it:

1. As you meditate, turn your attention to what it would feel like if you did truly accept yourself, exactly as you are. Think about how it would feel to experience full self-acceptance; you would probably be more ready to forgive yourself, to give yourself a break, and to replace negative with positive self-talk. You would also likely feel more confident and at peace with yourself and enjoy a healthy sense of self-esteem and self-respect.

2. Settle into these feelings and embrace them as the positive, uplifting feelings they are. Imagine yourself feeling like that. How would your behavior change? How would your inner monologue change?

3. However you think things would change, take some time to understand and incorporate these changes into your life. Start acting like you feel this way. You will find that acting like you accept yourself will soon lead to true self-acceptance.

VISUALIZE YOUR SUPPORT SYSTEM

Have you ever taken the time to visualize your support system? If you haven't, this exercise is an excellent way to start! Visualizing your support system is a great way to remind yourself of all the love in your life, to identify sources of support when you might need it, and even to learn to accept yourself more fully.

Here's what you do:

1. Visualize a large empty space around you, like a conference room, a basketball court, or a large meadow. See it in as much detail as you can.
2. Now think about the people who love you most. This might be your parent(s), grandparents, siblings, spouse, children, or intimate friends. Visualize each of them popping into existence in your space.
3. Cast your net a bit wider and think about whom you can definitely lean on in tough times, like your extended family, your friends, or your mentor or close colleague. Watch as they appear in your field of vision as well.
4. Now cast your net the widest, catching everyone whom you have appreciated as a source of support and care when times were tough. See all of them materialize in your space.
5. Looking over this veritable sea of faces, remind yourself that each and every one of them loves you for who you are and accepts you as you are. Ask yourself, "If they can accept me as I am, why can't I?" and commit to doing exactly that.

MOURN YOUR LOSSES
WHEN YOU NEED TO

Self-acceptance is a lifelong journey. Some days it will be easier, other days it might be a little more difficult; however, it's vital to learn how to push through during difficult times. If you've ever failed to reach a goal or experienced a big personal loss, it can be tough to accept your new reality. Maybe you didn't get into the program you've dreamed about attending for years, or perhaps you learned that you can't pursue your dream career because of something you can't change (e.g., poor eyesight keeping you from being a pilot). This meditation will help you learn how to push through the fog and accept yourself, even if you have to give up on some of your dreams to do it.

1. Think about your recent loss or failure and the new reality you need to accept. It may be painful at the moment, but don't worry—you'll feel better!

2. Spend a few minutes thinking about the future that you won't have. Mourn for your loss and give yourself some compassion and a small dose of self-pity.

3. When you've had time to thoroughly mourn your loss, imagine flipping a light switch in your mind. The light goes off over the doors that have closed, and the lights go on over the new doors you have to pick from. Set down the self-pity and imagine yourself walking through one of the new doors to a new future that's just as positive as the one you left behind.

PRACTICE ACCEPTANCE
OF OTHERS FIRST

Accepting yourself is vital to a happy and healthy life. However, it's a journey, not a destination. If you have trouble accepting yourself right away, try working on your acceptance of others first. This meditation will show you how to translate that acceptance of others into acceptance of yourself.

This is how it works:

1. Think of a few people in your life that you truly cherish and appreciate. Pick one of them and imagine having a conversation in which they tell you they don't feel accepted and valued.
2. Imagine what your response to them would be. You would likely reassure them of their worth as a person, remind them of their strengths, and share what you love about them.
3. Have this conversation in your head, listing all of the reasons why they should be more self-accepting. Write down these reasons if it will help you remember them.
4. Now, turn it around. Apply all of these reasons for self-acceptance to yourself. Remind yourself that your loved one should accept themselves as the wonderful human being they are for the same reason you should accept yourself: You are a flawed but good person who is doing your best.

Turning acceptance of others into acceptance of yourself is a powerful tactic that basically allows you to trick your brain into self-acceptance. Give it a try and see if it works for you!

ACTIVATE YOUR MOST ACTUALIZED SELF

If you've ever read about Maslow and the hierarchy of needs, you'll be familiar with the concept of your "actualized self." If not, here's a quick definition: Actualization is the pinnacle human need after other needs have been met (survival, belonging, etc.) and is achieved through becoming the best version of yourself that you can be. It's about using your talents and skills in a way that fulfills you. If you haven't quite reached this level yet, don't worry! You can still work with it to further your self-acceptance and self-love.

1. Picture yourself in your mind's eye, but make a few tweaks; visualize your *best possible* self, one that has embraced all your strengths and good qualities and uses them in a positive way.
2. Think about your actualized self. What do you love about him or her? What do you think makes this the best version of yourself?
3. Now remind yourself that this version is inside you right now and can be activated with some dedicated effort. Think of what you would like to incorporate from this best self into your own life. Commit to working toward this goal.
4. Whenever you have trouble meeting a goal or coping with challenges, remember that your best self is always inside you, ready to be activated anytime!

ACCEPT THAT WE'RE ALL DOING THE BEST WE CAN

One of the best lessons you can learn is a simple but powerful idea: We are all just doing the best we can with the tools we have at our disposal. We don't always apply this idea to ourselves, or we may fail to apply it to others by thinking about how we would handle a situation differently than others have handled it. While it's probably true that we would respond differently, we don't always realize that we all have different levels of knowledge, different resources, and different tactics. Use this meditation to remind yourself that we're all doing the best we can, and apply this idea to yourself as well as others.

1. Repeat this sentence to yourself a few times: "We are all doing the best we can with what we have."
2. Think about what it really means. Essentially, it's saying that with the exact same genetics, experience, and knowledge that you have, anyone in your shoes would make similar decisions and face similar challenges, successes, and defeats.
3. Consider what this means for others: They are doing their best and are deserving of acceptance and compassion. Next, consider what this means for you: You are doing the best you can with what you have and you are *also* deserving of acceptance and compassion.

Keep this lesson tucked away in your mind, and pull it out periodically to nudge yourself toward self-acceptance.

CHAPTER 2

MEDITATIONS ON SELF-APPRECIATION

Once you have a base of self-knowledge and self-acceptance, self-appreciation is the next layer to build in your pyramid of self-compassion. Self-appreciation takes the acceptance you've built a step further: Not only do you accept yourself as you are, but you also actively choose to appreciate, congratulate, and love yourself as you are. If you're feeling hung up on your flaws or down about your weaknesses and thinking this chapter isn't for you, know that this chapter is designed with you in mind. You don't need to feel 100 percent happy with yourself to appreciate yourself, but you can take practical, effective steps toward feeling happier with yourself overall. This chapter will introduce you to several ways to do just that, including celebrating your successes, focusing on your strengths, looking back over your past, appreciating your present self, anticipating your future self, altering your perspective, and treating yourself like a dear friend.

CONGRATULATE YOURSELF

Self-compassion becomes almost second nature when you make a habit of celebrating yourself. For most people it's relatively easy to appreciate others and show them that appreciation, but it can feel awkward or uncomfortable to extend the same appreciation to ourselves; however, it's vital to your well-being! You must first learn how to think kindly of yourself before you can feel true compassion for yourself.

If you have a hard time thinking kindly about yourself, this is the perfect meditation for you. To give it a try, follow these steps:

1. Prepare yourself for meditation, then center yourself by taking five deep breaths, inhaling for three seconds and exhaling for three seconds.

2. Bring to mind a few of your successes. These can be large-scale successes, like establishing a business, or they can be smaller, day-to-day successes, like making it to the gym a certain number of days this week.

3. Cultivate appreciation for the hard work that went into your success, and let that appreciation expand past the borders of your examples and into a more general sense of appreciation for yourself.

4. Either out loud or in your head, tell yourself something encouraging, like, "Great job!" or, "Congratulations on being a successful adult!" It might seem silly at first, but you'll find that you probably like being congratulated—even by yourself!

LIST YOUR STRENGTHS

It's wonderful to be able to appreciate yourself without prompting or encouragement, but sometimes you need a little push to get in a self-appreciation state of mind. When you feel the need for that bit of encouragement, consider your strengths. Whether or not you believe you have any special skills or talents, you undoubtedly have strengths! We all have strengths (and weaknesses, but we often find those easier to identify), and we can pull from these strengths to get us through difficult times. We can also use them to remind ourselves of why we deserve our own love and compassion.

Here's how to practice a strengths-focused meditation:

1. Grab a journal and prepare for meditation as you normally do.
2. Focus your awareness on yourself. Recall a few examples of times when you've succeeded, especially if your success was unexpected or hard-won.
3. Think about what these examples show. Are there patterns? Can you see any repeat behaviors in your successes? For instance, you might notice that you tend to procrastinate but can work well under pressure.
4. Once you have a few strengths identified, write them down. Keep going for as long as you can think of strengths, then put your pen down and read through the list.
5. Give yourself a pat on the back and congratulate yourself for these things that you do well.

THANK YOUR PAST SELF

We are all humans, meaning we are all uniquely and beautifully flawed—we have all made mistakes, regretted our actions, and wished we could go back and change things. It's natural to look back on our past selves with a focus on the negative, but it's not always helpful. If you haven't taken the time to look back on your past self and appreciate who you were, this exercise is a great way to give that a try.

1. When you're ready to get started, take another deep breath to center yourself. Shift your focus from your breath to your past.
2. Pick a point in time in your past when you were going through a difficult transition or making a tough choice. Think about what you were doing and how you were feeling at the time. Remember how tough it was to be in that situation.
3. Now, remember what it felt like to pull through. Think about how you handled the situation or made the decision. Relive the experience of figuring things out, getting things back on track, or whatever else you did that made a success out of your situation.
4. Congratulate yourself on a job well done, then craft an earnest thank-you note (either on paper or in your head). Put some thought and detail into your note, and word it in such a way that "past you" would have been thrilled to receive it.

CELEBRATE YOUR CURRENT SELF

If you are able to celebrate yourself, it's much easier to have compassion for yourself when times get tough. Don't worry; celebrating yourself isn't about being vain, arrogant, or narcissistic. It's about being realistic and giving yourself the recognition and respect that you would give to any loved one. Keep your celebration honest and earnest, and you will reap the benefits of your self-appreciation.

Here's how to celebrate your current self:

1. After prepping for your meditation session, shift your focus to yourself. Think about who you are, right here, right now.
2. Bring to your awareness a few very recent examples of catching yourself practicing good behavior. It could be something as small as keeping your cool when someone cut you off in traffic, or keeping a less-than-charitable comment to yourself when your coworkers were gossiping.
3. Think about what these examples say about you. What larger character traits do they point to? What are you proud of that you do well? Identify these traits and strengths.
4. Embrace these examples of your good nature and take a few minutes to bask in the good feelings. Celebrate the positive things you do and the positive traits behind them. Remind yourself that it's okay to love yourself and feel good about who you are.

ANTICIPATE YOUR FUTURE SELF

It's a great practice to learn how to appreciate yourself—*truly* appreciate yourself—but if you want to kick your practice up a notch, try something a bit more challenging: appreciating your *future* self. We often spend time daydreaming about what our life will be like in the future, whether it's once we get that job we want, once we're happily married, or when we have a house full of children to delight in. Take advantage of this natural inclination to look toward the future and give yourself a boost of self-appreciation.

1. Once you're prepared to meditate, fix your internal gaze on yourself at a certain point in the future. It can be near or very far away (that part doesn't matter), but it must be at a time when you can see yourself being happy and healthy.
2. Focus on yourself at this point in time. Try to get yourself in this future self's mindset, and think about all the things that will have changed. Imagine what you will have accomplished by that time and how you will feel.
3. Gather up all these feelings of accomplishment and put them toward appreciating your future self.

This exercise has the added bonus of helping you visualize yourself completing any important and personally meaningful goals you might have, which will make you even more proud of yourself!

SEE YOURSELF FROM A LOVED ONE'S PERSPECTIVE

When you're having trouble appreciating yourself, there's a tried-and-true method that can help you get in the right frame of mind: thinking of yourself from the perspective of someone who loves you. It's easy for us to appreciate our friends and family. We can so easily list their good qualities and positive traits, because we see them so clearly; however, our view can get a little fuzzy when we're trying to identify and appreciate our own strengths. If you aren't feeling very self-appreciative, give this meditation a try.

1. When you're ready to get started, focus your attention on yourself, but pull back a bit. Instead of seeing yourself as you usually do, put on a different lens; imagine seeing yourself through the eyes of your closest friends and family.
2. Think about what your loved ones appreciate about you. If it helps, you can make a list of these qualities. Remind yourself that these traits make you a wonderful person and a great friend or family member to those you love.
3. Wrap yourself in their love and acceptance, and use it to add to your own sense of self-acceptance. Even on your worst day, remember that there are good reasons that the people in your life love you.

CHIP AWAY
AT THE WALL

If you're like many people who occasionally struggle with their mental health, you are probably familiar with the concept of the wall. It's an internal wall that we erect between our conscious, rational selves and our authentic, emotional inner selves; it's what keeps the logical and reasonable side of our brain from truly seeing and appreciating ourselves for who we are, even when there is a ton of good there to appreciate. The wall is not healthy or helpful, but it can be difficult to tear it down. Don't expect to demolish the wall all at once, but you can establish a practice of chipping away at the wall that stands between you and self-appreciation.

Here's how:

1. When you're prepared to meditate, begin with a visualization. Imagine there is a literal wall in your mind; on one side of the wall is your practical, totally reasonable self and on the other is your vulnerable inner self.
2. Take a look at this wall. Notice that it's made of insults, faulty assumptions, and unhealthy core beliefs. This wall is a visual representation of the obstacles between you and self-appreciation.
3. In your head, grab a sledgehammer or pickaxe and choose a spot where the wall looks weakest, like a silly self-criticism that you know isn't based in truth or an old wound that just doesn't hurt as much anymore. Attack this spot with your weapon of choice and watch the wall begin to crumble!

IMAGINE YOURSELF AS THE PROTAGONIST

Do you find it easy to identify with the protagonist in a book, movie, or TV show? You most likely do, at least with stories that you enjoy and become immersed in. The protagonist is specifically written to make most people identify with them, and they always have at least a few positive traits.

If you find it difficult to appreciate yourself but easily identify with the main characters in your favorite stories, consider seeing yourself as a protagonist. Follow these steps to give this meditation a try:

1. When you're feeling centered and ready to meditate, pull back a bit and begin to put together a bird's-eye view of your life.

2. Think of some of your biggest challenges that you have overcome. If it helps, you can write them down in a notebook to cement them in your mind or put together a timeline.

3. Dramatize your life! Think about how you felt when you accomplished a major goal, but imagine it as if it were a movie scene. For example, take graduating from college: Imagine a triumphant scene where you take the stage with confidence, get meaningful nods of approval from the faculty, and visualize a perfect slow-motion experience of receiving your diploma.

4. Repeat this for your biggest achievements and put together a mini movie in your head. Watch the movie and allow yourself to feel pride and joy for the protagonist, then give yourself a pat on the back for *being* that protagonist.

TREAT YOURSELF
LIKE A FRIEND

This meditation is similar to the See Yourself from a Loved One's Perspective meditation earlier in this chapter, but it actually flips the concept: Instead of seeing yourself through someone else's eyes, you'll work on changing how *you* look at yourself. Follow these steps to give it a try and see if you can give yourself a fresh new perspective:

1. Once you're ready to get started, take another two or three deep, calming breaths to get centered.
2. Picture yourself in your mind's eye. See yourself as you really are, but focus on the best parts of you. Think of yourself laughing, telling a joke, sharing your love for your partner or a dear friend, or doing something that makes you proud.
3. Try to detach yourself from the person you see. View them as you would a friend, with a friend's caring eye. Notice all the good things about this person and cultivate appreciation for them.
4. Tell this new friend how you feel about them. You can do it out loud, in your head, or in your journal. If you're not sure what to say, try these expressions of appreciation:

   * "I love you and I appreciate you."
   * "I see you, I know you, and I accept you."
   * "You are worthy of love and respect."
   * "You are a great person and an excellent friend."

GIVE YOURSELF THE BENEFIT OF THE DOUBT

If you're like many people, you frequently find yourself giving people the benefit of the doubt. It can be easy to make excuses—whether real or not, and whether deserved or not—for other people when an issue arises. For example, if someone is running late to a meeting with you, you might assume they got caught in traffic, or their kids were making it difficult to get out of the house, or maybe they're just overwhelmed by life right now. On the other hand, if you are running late, you might jump immediately to thoughts like, "This was so rude of me" or "I am terrible at managing my time." While it's not bad to hold yourself accountable, it's a good idea to practice giving yourself the benefit of the doubt.

1. After prepping for your meditation, take another moment or two to clear your head and start fresh. When you're ready, think of a recent incident in which you felt bad about something you did (or didn't) do.
2. Think about how you felt about yourself during or after the incident, and identify any blame you placed on yourself.
3. Now imagine someone you respect made the same mistake. Consider the possibilities you would come up with to excuse or mitigate their behavior, and apply these excuses to yourself.
4. Take a deep breath and let out any lingering shame or guilt, and commit to giving yourself the benefit of the doubt more often.

PRACTICE
SELF-KINDNESS

It feels great to be the recipient of kindness. Sometimes all it takes is someone holding a door open for you or picking up something you dropped to change your mindset and make you more appreciative. Generally, these acts of kindness make you appreciate the person on the giving end, but here's a little secret: You can benefit from being both the giver *and* the receiver of your own kindness!

Here's how to do it:

1. Think of kind things that people have done for you. These acts of kindness could include complimenting you on your performance in a work presentation, buying you a coffee or tea on a low day, or even just waving you in when you needed to switch lanes in busy traffic.

2. Come up with at least five or six examples, then think about whether you can do these things for yourself. You can't wave yourself into a lane in traffic, of course, but there should be other things! For example, you could buy yourself a coffee if you need a little cheering up.

3. Think of how it makes you feel when people do these kind things for you, and practice cultivating that feeling for yourself when you are both the giver and the receiver. Open yourself up to it, and appreciate yourself for your own kind gestures.

IDENTIFY SELF-NEGATIVE THOUGHT PATTERNS

One of the best methods you have of boosting your self-acceptance and self-appreciation is to keep track of your thought patterns and make sure they are kind to yourself. We all have the capacity to be good to ourselves and overly negative about ourselves, and we also have the ability to improve our track record in this area. Practice this meditation to nip self-negative thoughts in the bud.

1. Stay quiet and relaxed after your meditation prep, but allow thoughts to roll in and out of your mind. Continue simply observing your thoughts until you find one that is negative toward yourself.

2. "Catch" this thought and examine it. What is the content? What is the tone? How is it worded? Explore this thought to see where it's coming from and what may have caused it. For example, maybe it's caused by your tendency to be overly harsh toward your own work, or perhaps it comes from a leftover bit of guilt about hurting someone you love.

3. Wherever it came from, commit to noticing this thought and others like it when they pop up. Instead of allowing them to come and go in your mind as they please, stop them in their tracks and question them. Think back to the root cause and realize that these thoughts are not based in reality.

Practice this exercise often!

PRACTICE
POSITIVE SELF-TALK

It's really helpful to your sense of self-appreciation and self-compassion to identify and neutralize negative self-talk, but it's important to also practice purposefully positive self-talk; although an absence of negative thoughts is great, it's not enough to help you build true self-love! To work on your positive self-talk, try this meditation exercise.

1. Begin by thinking about what you like about yourself. Call to mind at least a few things that you have noticed you receive compliments on or things that you are proud of. These could be anything you're good at, ranging from excelling at completing puzzles to cooking a mean pot roast to driving a stick-shift car.

2. Think of at least a few compliments based on these strengths or skills of yours. For instance, if you are proud of your ability to solve puzzles, you might come up with something like "You are so quick and efficient at solving puzzles!" or "Your mind is so sharp!"

3. Practice saying these compliments out loud, and practice accepting them with grace. Repeat them a few times each to get used to them and let the compliments sink in.

4. Here's the most important part: Let yourself believe them. Give in to the onslaught of compliments, and you will find that you start thinking of yourself in a much more positive light.

REFUSE TO APOLOGIZE
(FOR BEING YOU)

This meditation is all about refusing to be ashamed or apologetic for being who you are. If you've never heard of the singer Lizzo before, I recommend that you look her up; she's a talented, hardworking, and unapologetic woman who refuses to feel shame for who she is, and her songs reflect that. If you need a little extra motivation to be un-apologetically you, put on one of her tracks and let it encourage you. If you're already motivated—or you already have all of Lizzo's songs memorized—you can jump right into the meditation!

1. Prep for your meditation with an extra focus on being in a comfortable seat and a strong pose. You could try lifting your chin up a little higher, sitting a little straighter, or even "posing" in a classic power pose.

2. Think about your little flaws that nag at you or times when you've failed and basically wanted to apologize to everyone around you. Consider how small these things are in the grand scheme of things. Ask yourself whether you really have time to be embarrassed or ashamed of something so inconsequential.

3. Decide that you don't need to apologize for not being perfect. Refuse to apologize for being your authentic self, even if that makes others jealous or upset.

4. Wrap yourself in self-love and self-appreciation and commit to embracing the experience of being you.

PRACTICE
SAYING NO

Many people find that the simple act of saying no can be the most empowering thing they've done. Lots of us feel like we can't say no without experiencing guilt or shame. It's understandable to feel this way, but these feelings are not based in reality. The sooner you learn how to say no, the sooner you will learn to appreciate yourself.

1. Think about a recent scenario in which you said yes but really wanted to or felt that you should have said no. It might have been during an interaction with a needy coworker or a conversation with a friend that doesn't respect boundaries.

2. Think about why you said yes when you really wanted to say no. Dive deep! Is it because you feel that it's rude to say no? Or were you afraid of losing your friend's affections if you said no?

3. Whatever your reason(s), remind yourself that it's perfectly healthy and okay to say no when you need to. Remember the instructions you receive on the airplane about putting on your own oxygen mask before helping someone else with their mask? That idea applies here: You need to be in a good mental place before you can give to others.

4. Relive this scenario, but say no instead of yes. Repeat this a few times. Visualize the scene going perfectly fine—no anger or disappointment—and commit to saying no more often.

CHAPTER 3

MEDITATIONS ON MEETING YOUR EMOTIONS

One of the most important things you can do to improve your self-compassion is to work on meeting your emotions. This refers to your capacity to notice your emotions, identify them, and effectively cope with or embrace them. Because they are a natural and normal part of human nature, you can't avoid having emotions. Throughout your life you will feel a lot of emotions: good ones, "bad" ones, and everything in between. Learning to accept and work with your emotions will make it much easier to cope with the challenges of everyday life and become a happier and healthier version of yourself. In this chapter, you will take several different tacks to meeting your emotions, including accepting the less pleasant emotions (like sadness and anger), seeking out more positive emotions (like joy), finding ways to deal with rumination and shame, and meditating on your emotional experiences.

ACCEPT
YOUR SADNESS

Although being sad is one of the not-so-great experiences in life, it's one that is not only inevitable but also necessary and healthy. From an evolutionary perspective, sadness prompts behaviors that contribute to our survival as a species, but it is also necessary to help us identify what we value and what we need. Further, experiencing sadness makes the experience of joy even sweeter!

Still, knowing this and accepting your sadness are two different things. Try this meditation to accept your sadness.

1. Find the sadness that you are carrying and let it out of the cage you have in your mind to contain it. Allow it to take center stage in your mind. It's alright if you shed a tear or two (or even more), so don't try to hold yourself back.

2. Sit with the sadness. Allow yourself to feel it. Don't try to deny or bury the sadness; simply let it flow.

3. Identify the source of your sadness, and think about what the sadness is doing for you or what it really represents. For example, if you're sad because a relationship just ended, remind yourself that sadness is appropriate and shows that you really cared for the other person.

4. Let yourself be sad for a few minutes. Accept the sadness and what it represents.

5. Finally, pull yourself out of the sadness by thinking about something a little brighter. You want to accept your sadness, but not let it overtake you.

FIND
YOUR JOY

Accepting your emotions isn't all about making peace with the negative ones, although that is certainly important; it's also about accepting and inviting in the positive emotions. For a variety of reasons, we sometimes have trouble accepting positive emotions. Whether it's depression, anxiety, guilt, or simply a pessimistic personality, there are lots of things that can make us hesitant to be happy. If this rings true for you, give this exercise a try.

1. Prepare for meditation as you usually do, but start out with a gentle smile on your face. Try to maintain that smile throughout your meditation prep.

2. When you're ready to get started, begin by thinking about how it feels to smile. What emotions come up when you smile? What does it make you feel?

3. Now move on to thinking about what makes you smile. Think of a few times when you've felt pure, unadulterated joy. You might have to think back to when you were a kid, and that's okay! Childhood is the easiest time to find joy like this.

4. Capture that joy and hang onto it. Let it sink into and permeate every pore. Embrace the feeling of joy and use this as a reminder of what it feels like, especially if you haven't felt it in a while.

5. Tell yourself that you deserve to feel this joy. Allow yourself to enjoy it and remind yourself to be open to it whenever you get an opportunity to feel joy.

ACCEPT
YOUR ANGER

Even the most mellow and easygoing among us get angry sometimes. It's a natural and normal part of being human! However, if you're prone to getting angry on a regular basis, you could probably benefit from accepting your anger and working with it. This meditation will help you accept your emotions, which will make it easier to accept yourself and give yourself some compassion.

1. Bring to mind the last time you got uncomfortably angry. It could be earlier today, last week, or last year, whatever is most salient.

2. Remember how it felt to be angry. Don't focus on what caused the anger so much, but on what you experienced. Did you shake? Turn red? Clam up? Do some unintentional word vomiting?

3. Allow yourself to feel it all over again, but with one change: Instead of letting your anger consume you, simply allow it to be. Let yourself feel angry, but stay nonjudgmental.

4. Sit with your anger for a few minutes, then choose to let it go. Watch it drift away in your mind, as if it were being swept away like a cloud in a breeze.

5. Remind yourself that it's normal and it's okay to feel angry, but that you have a choice in how you deal with your anger. Commit to choosing to react in the same nonjudgmental, emotion-accepting way you did today.

PLAN FOR
YOUR ANGER

When you have a strong emotional reaction, it's easy to get swept away in the moment; however, when you have a plan for how to respond to such an event, it's easier to stay focused and respond in a way that you feel more comfortable with. If you ever say or do things you regret when you get angry, then you may want to work on being more than just observant of your anger; you will likely benefit from *planning* for your anger.

This exercise will help you practice and prepare you for your next rendezvous with anger.

1. Think about a situation that would provoke anger in you. Allow yourself to feel your anger and accept your anger.
2. Next, pay attention to what you feel and what you want to do when you're angry. Note your response to anger, such as shaking hands, a desire to yell at someone, or an urge to punch a wall.
3. Think about what would distract you or defuse the tension. If you feel like acting out physically, consider throwing a pillow at your couch instead. If you feel like letting out a string of obscenities, try counting backward from ten.
4. Find something that works for you and practice it a few times. Allow yourself to become angry and use the technique you identified.
5. If the technique fails the first couple times, don't get upset with yourself! Show yourself compassion. If it still doesn't work after a few attempts, consider another technique.

WORK THROUGH INTENSE EMOTIONS

If you find yourself frequently getting swept up in strong emotions, you probably find it frustrating. You might feel like you don't have any control over how you feel in times like these, but the truth is that you do have the ability to influence your feelings in an indirect route; you can't simply stop feeling a certain way, but you can respond to your emotion in such a way that brings you out of your negative emotion.

Here's how:

1. Think about a scenario that generally leads you to feel out of control and consumed by an emotion. Sink into it and let yourself get a taste of how you would feel.

2. Based on this taste, think about how you could neutralize the strong feelings without denying or actively fighting them. For example, if you tend to get swept up in sadness when something important goes wrong, consider taking an action that you would have taken if things went right (e.g., if you would have celebrated, take yourself out to a nice dinner anyway).

3. When you act like you don't feel sad, it can trick your brain into thinking you're not really sad, and that can get you right back to emotional equilibrium. You're not fighting your feelings; you're just not letting them dictate your behavior.

Use this meditation to work through any intense emotion you might feel, and you will find that it's much easier to accept yourself and your emotions for what they are.

ANTICIPATE
YOUR NEEDS

One of the most wonderful experiences in a relationship is when a partner anticipates your needs and acts accordingly. For example, if your partner realizes that you tend to need some alone time when you get home from work, they might purposely give you a kiss and make you your favorite beverage when you get home, but avoid asking about your day for a half an hour or so. It's wonderful to feel so cared for and taken care of! You might not have considered this before, but you can actually give this gift to yourself too.

Here's a guide to anticipating and satisfying your own needs:

1. Think about occasions when you often feel an intense need for something. For instance, you might identify with the previous example and need some alone time after a hard day's work. Or you might know that you always want some pampering after you do a particularly tough chore, like cleaning the whole house.

2. Now, identify what would help you meet this need. In the tough chore example, maybe a scheduled massage for the evening after you clean would meet your needs. Whatever it is, make a plan to meet the needs that you are anticipating.

3. Give yourself a pat on the back for working to anticipate your needs and accepting your emotions as they come!

MEDITATE ON
YOUR PAST EMOTIONS

One excellent method of working with and accepting your emotions is to meditate on your past emotional experiences. You don't need to schedule a retrospective for every instance of emotional engagement you've experienced, but taking time to reflect on your emotional experiences, particularly the more intense ones, can be helpful.

If you're not sure how to get started meditating on your past emotions, give this exercise a try:

1. Prepare to meditate as you usually do, but add in a few more deep breaths at the end. This is a good idea whenever you are about to engage your more emotional side, as it helps you get centered and clear your mind of internal baggage.
2. Call to mind a recent experience with a strong emotion. It can be a "good" experience or a "bad" experience; it just needs to be a strong one.
3. Think about how you felt during this experience. Go through each of the emotions you experienced and remember exactly how it felt (or in as much detail as possible).
4. Think about how you felt *after* this experience, whether that was feeling cleansed and refreshed, exhausted, or upbeat.
5. Accept that intense emotions are a normal part of life, and cultivate a sense of gratitude for the good ones and the bad ones alike. Commit to remembering this the next time you feel an intense emotion.

CHECK IN WITH
YOUR PRESENT EMOTIONS

How are you feeling right now, in this very moment?

That's a question you may not ask yourself very often, but it can be extremely beneficial to your well-being if you make it a habit. We tend not to think too much about how we are feeling unless how we are feeling is particularly poignant (e.g., feeling ecstatic, intensely sad, livid), but checking in with your present emotions is an effective way to get in touch with yourself and accept yourself as you are.

Here's how to check in with your present emotions via meditation:

1. Once you're prepared, continue to breathe deeply for a few more moments. Then come into stillness and ask yourself, "How do I feel?" You can ask yourself in your head, out loud, or even write it down if that feels natural.

2. Pause and give some thought to how you feel. You are almost certainly feeling more than one emotion, so dig deep! Humans are complex creatures that can harbor many different emotions at once.

3. Tap into each emotion you identified. Explore it, sample it, and get to know it. Become familiar with your experience of each emotion so you can more easily label it next time it pops up.

4. Promise yourself that you'll check in with your emotions at least once more today.

This meditation will boost your emotional intelligence and help you prepare yourself to effectively accept and address your emotions.

UNCONDITIONALLY ACCEPT YOUR FUTURE EMOTIONS

This meditation is more challenging than simply accepting your present emotions, but it's a great way to boost your emotional intelligence and encourage self-acceptance and, in turn, self-compassion. It also gives you a chance to practice visualization and forward thinking.

Follow these instructions to work on accepting your future emotions:

1. After your meditation prep, turn your attention toward the future. Think about at least a few big events you have coming up, like a wedding, a vacation, or even something difficult, like a court date.

2. Think about how you will probably feel during these future events. Consider how strongly you will feel these emotions and what else they will prompt in you (e.g., desires to engage in particular activities or behaviors, lead-ins to other emotions).

3. Tell yourself that you will probably experience these feelings and urges in the future, and that's okay. Even when you know situations like these are coming, you can't always ward off the emotions that come with them. For example, you will likely cry at your child's wedding; you know it, and you may try to fight off the tears, but they will probably find a way out anyway!

4. Tell yourself that there's nothing wrong with feeling these emotions in the future—or any other emotions. All of your feelings are valid, so commit to unconditionally accepting your future emotions and meeting them with open arms, even if they're not the most pleasant ones.

ALLOW YOURSELF TO FEEL

If you're someone who avoids getting too involved in movies, TV shows, or books with strong emotional elements, you may have a small aversion to feeling. It's fine if you're simply not a very emotional person, but an issue can arise if you eventually *do* feel something strongly, and you don't really know how to handle it! Instead of letting yourself get caught off guard, allow yourself to practice feeling and get used to the experience.

Here's how to do it:

1. Think about the most intensely emotional plotline or story you have heard. Consider which character you most easily identified with, and dig a little deeper into them.

2. Put yourself in this character's mindset, and imagine how it would feel to be in their shoes. Instead of pulling away as you usually might, allow the experience to expand. Spend a few minutes on this, really sinking into the story.

3. Make note of the emotions that you feel. You can write them down in a journal if that helps you identify and label them. Accept that you are currently feeling each of these emotions.

4. Now, purposefully let them go. Watch them drift away in your mind's eye, like a leaf on a gently flowing river.

5. Finish the meditation by telling yourself that, despite feeling uncomfortably strong emotions, you are okay. Remind yourself that you are separate from your emotions but can never really escape them—and that you don't need to.

NEUTRALIZE
YOUR RUMINATION

Do you ever ruminate? Rumination is a natural, if unpleasant, part of having thoughts and emotions; however, just because it's natural doesn't mean it's healthy. If you find yourself ruminating on a regular basis—or just too often for your own comfort—this meditation can help you neutralize it.

1. When you catch yourself ruminating, hit the pause button and stop what you're doing immediately. Prepare yourself for meditation however you normally do.

2. Continue breathing deeply and slowly after you get yourself prepped, and work on clearing your mind of any unnecessary "filler" stuff.

3. Capture a few of those ruminating thoughts and isolate them. Pull them out of the context and see them as stand-alone thoughts. When you do, you'll likely notice how silly or pointless they are. For example, one ruminating thought might be, "If only I could go back and have that conversation again with the knowledge I have now."

4. Point out the flaws in your own ruminations. For example, you might make some notes like this about the previous thought: "I can't go back in time, so thinking about what I would do now is pointless. The other person probably doesn't even remember that conversation. If I had the knowledge I have now, I probably wouldn't have even entered that conversation."

5. Remind yourself of the futility of ruminating. Accept your emotions for what they are, but know that you can influence your thought patterns, even if it feels impossible at times.

REJECT
FEELINGS OF SHAME

Have you ever heard about the difference between guilt and shame? If not, there is a valuable lesson to be learned in this quick dictionary dive. Although they feel similar, they are based on different core beliefs and driven by two very separate ideas: Guilt is driven by a mindset of "I feel bad about what I did," and shame is driven by a mindset of "I feel bad about who I am." It's perfectly fine and healthy to feel guilty when you make a mistake, but there is nothing healthy about feeling shame for honest mistakes.

Here's how to address those sneaky feelings of shame:

1. Think of the action (or lack of action) you engaged in recently that brought feelings of shame. Identify what felt shameful, and why it felt shameful.

2. Think about how you would lovingly counsel a friend or family member who made the same mistake. Think about why it is so easy to forgive someone you love for this action: It's possible at least in part because you can separate the mistake from the person you love. You know they did it, but you see them as more than just one act.

3. Now, apply that same logic to yourself. Allow that you did something regrettable, but that one thing doesn't define you. Assuming this conduct is not a felony or a truly heinous action, it should be easy enough to separate the behavior from the individual.

MEDITATE ON WHAT IT MEANS TO BE HUMAN

What does it really mean to be human? That's a big question, isn't it? Philosophers can argue about it all day, but for our purposes we can boil it down to a few points: Being human means that we are (1) complex, (2) emotional, and (3) fallible creatures. Not a single one of us is one-dimensional, nor do any of us live a life free of emotion. And, of course, no one is perfect. These are three defining features of being human, but sometimes we still forget them. Use this meditation to remind yourself of what it means to be human.

1. When you're ready to meditate, bring to mind these three features of being human. You can write them down if that helps. Remind yourself that, as a member of the human race, you are complex, emotional, and fallible.

2. Remind yourself that you are not one-dimensional, nor are you defined by one or two traits or characteristics. You have tons of traits, many good, some not so good, but they are all a part of you.

3. Remind yourself that you are emotional by nature, and there's nothing wrong with that. We all have emotions, sometimes very strong emotions, and that's okay.

4. Remind yourself that you are fallible. You are not perfect, nor are you expected to be.

5. Accept these facts as the inevitable, inescapable truths of life that they are. Give yourself a purposeful break for each of these features, and show yourself a little love.

ACCEPT THE UNCERTAINTY OF VULNERABILITY

Being vulnerable can be scary, but it's also the key to living a life that makes all the hard times worth it. To be vulnerable is to be self-accepting, secure in who you are, and open to experiencing all that this world has to offer. It can be scary, but it's the only way to truly get to know yourself and let others get to know the real you. To work on accepting this idea and being more vulnerable, try this meditation.

1. Keeping your eyes closed, think about what life would be like without vulnerability. Imagine you were impervious to any kind of emotional pain or insecurity. It probably sounds great on the surface, but think about how much less exciting, challenging, and fulfilling life would be.

2. Would you cherish your successes as much? Would you appreciate the intimacy you share with your loved ones as much? The answer is most likely no.

3. Tell yourself that being vulnerable is the secret ingredient to a life of authentic happiness. Vulnerability is not a weakness; it is actually our greatest strength when wielded appropriately.

4. Accept that you cannot plan for and control everything, and that sometimes you will get hurt. However, remind yourself that you would miss out on the best moments in life if you never allowed yourself to be vulnerable. Commit to measured, open-minded vulnerability moving forward.

CULTIVATE A SENSE
OF CHILDLIKE WONDER

Think about most children you know. Would you say they are stable and emotionally savvy individuals? Probably not—children are not known for their emotional intelligence and predictable moods! While it can be frustrating at times, their openness to their emotions is also related to one of their most wonderful features: childlike wonder. Some of this natural wonder evaporates as we grow and gain knowledge and experience, but we don't need to let it *all* go. Try this meditation to get some of that childlike wonder back.

1. Think about what it felt like to see something wonderful or amazing as a child. Remember what it was like to be totally consumed by awe, whether it was over a house decorated with Christmas lights or one of the Seven Wonders of the World.

2. Embrace that feeling of wonder and awe. Remind yourself of how it felt to be completely overwhelmed by raw positive emotion, and give yourself permission to feel that way again.

3. Take a look around you with this childlike perspective. What is amazing and wonderful and spectacular in your immediate environment? If you can't think of anything nearby, extend your search a bit further. For example, bring to mind the closest national park or the last intense thunderstorm you experienced.

4. Give in to the sense of wonder, cultivate it, and maintain it. Allow yourself to feel everything like it was the first time, and watch your sense of awe and wonder grow.

CHAPTER 4

MEDITATIONS ON SELF-FORGIVENESS

Self-compassion is impossible without self-forgiveness. Trying to build self-compassion without self-forgiveness would be like trying to bake chocolate chip cookies without any chocolate; sure, you'll get something *like* chocolate chip cookies, but you'll be missing the ingredient that really makes the cookies what they are. Self-forgiveness is the chocolate in your chocolate chip cookies; without it, do you even have self-compassion? You can work on accepting and loving and respecting yourself all day long (and you should work on these things!), but eventually you are going to fail or make a big mistake. When this happens, it's self-forgiveness that allows you to remain compassionate and loving with yourself. To work on your capacity to forgive yourself and maintain self-compassion even in the face of guilt, shame, and failure, check out the next fifteen meditations.

GIVE YOURSELF PERMISSION TO FORGIVE

Many of us struggle with forgiveness, both self-forgiveness and forgiveness of others. It can be especially difficult to forgive when we are feeling vulnerable. You might feel like you are enabling bad behavior or even encouraging it by forgiving others, but that's not true; forgiveness is simply saying that you are choosing to let go of emotions that are not serving you. It might take some practice, but you can learn to give yourself permission to forgive.

Here's how:

1. Prepare to meditate as usual, then shift your posture slightly by putting both hands over your heart. Take a moment to feel your heart beating and get in touch with its rhythm.

2. Think about the hurt that your heart has carried, hurt caused by others and by you. Remind yourself that pain is an inevitable part of life and that it's okay to feel pain.

3. Now, imagine that there is a barrier around your heart with a locked gate. The barrier prevents your heart from extending forgiveness—to yourself or to others—and the gate is firmly locked. This keeps some pain from getting in, but it also keeps compassion from getting out.

4. Take a deep breath and imagine a key in your hand. This key is a symbol of your permission to yourself to practice forgiveness.

5. Take the key and unlock the gate, gently swinging it open. Tell yourself that you are formally giving yourself permission to forgive, and allow your heart to feel free and open.

PRACTICE SELF-FORGIVENESS FOR SOMETHING SMALL

When you first practice self-forgiveness, it can be tough to start with something big; so, instead of putting pressure on yourself to forgive a big mistake, it's a good idea to start off small. It might not feel like you're making progress by forgiving yourself for something like leaving the milk out too long, but it helps you get in the right frame of mind and practice for the bigger stuff.

1. After your meditation prep, sit with the silence for a few moments and continue focusing on your breath. Allow thoughts to enter your mind but let them pass out just as easily. Avoid becoming attached to them.

2. Think of a recent mistake you made that's pretty low on the spectrum of "bad" behavior. Perhaps you made a small but thoughtless comment to a friend, or forgot to pay a bill on time.

3. Consider how this mistake made you feel; you might feel silly, ashamed of yourself, a little guilty, or even stupid. Make note of these feelings.

4. Remind yourself that these feelings are pretty intense for such a small blip on the radar of life, and that the consequences are not exactly dire. No irreparable harm was done, and it will likely be easy to rectify the mistake.

5. Tell yourself that to err is to be human, and that everyone makes mistakes. Disconnect the concept of your small mistake from your worth as a person, and extend to yourself the olive branch of forgiveness.

FORGIVE YOURSELF FOR A BIG MISTAKE

When you have some experience forgiving yourself for a small mistake (see the previous meditation if you haven't tried it yet), it might be time to move on to a larger mistake. Don't think that you need to jump into forgiving yourself for the biggest mistake you ever made; just choose a mistake that had bigger consequences than your small mistake. For example, you might have dropped the ball on a big project at work or forgotten something important to your partner. When you have the mistake in mind, prepare for meditation as you usually do, then follow these steps:

1. Think about the mistake you made and flesh it out in your mind or on paper. Consider where you made the misstep and why you made it. Think of what beliefs, values, or ideas drove you to the mistake.
2. Think about the repercussions of your mistake (e.g., getting a mediocre or even negative review at work, a big fight with your spouse), but also consider how the mistake was or could be rectified. It is likely not a lost cause!
3. Catalog your lesson(s) learned. Was there a positive takeaway from the experience?
4. Remind yourself that we all make mistakes, and that sometimes mistakes can lead to even better opportunities and greater personal development. Practice forgiving yourself for this mistake.

GIVE YOURSELF A BLANKET APOLOGY—AND ACCEPT IT

If you thought forgiving yourself for a large mistake was hard, this meditation will be an even bigger challenge—but bigger challenges produce greater benefits! Giving yourself what is called a "blanket apology" will put your self-forgiveness skills to the test and help you develop an even better habit of forgiving yourself for your transgressions.

Here's how to do it:

1. When you're ready, take a few extra slow, deep breaths and get centered. Prepare yourself to extend some serious compassion!
2. Think of a few of your mistakes. They can be big mistakes, recent mistakes, or any other salient examples that come to mind. Note them, but don't spend any time dwelling on them. Let them come into your head and just as quickly let them slide out.
3. Note how you feel when you think of your mistakes. You might feel sad, angry, ashamed, guilty, ignorant, understanding, or any of a combination of emotions. Whatever you are feeling is valid and okay.
4. However, just because it's okay to experience your feelings doesn't mean you should resign yourself to them. Instead of dwelling on your past mistakes, offer yourself a blanket apology. This apology absolves you of the guilt for each and every one of your mistakes, leaving you guilt-free and unburdened.
5. Accept the apology. Write down your acceptance if you need to; just make sure to spend a few moments truly receiving and accepting the apology.

PUT YOURSELF IN A FRIEND'S SHOES

If you often have trouble extending forgiveness to yourself, you may want to try this meditation. It takes some of the mental load off and gives you a way to more easily slide into self-forgiveness if this practice doesn't come naturally to you.

Here's how to put yourself in a friend's shoes to boost your capacity for self-forgiveness:

1. When you're ready to meditate, bring a dear friend to mind. This should be somebody that loves you and regularly displays that love for you.

2. Think of a mistake or silly thing you did recently that you are beating yourself up over. Gather all the details in your head or on paper so that you have a full understanding of it.

3. Now think about how that friend would feel knowing you are experiencing prolonged guilt for one mistake. Imagine you are talking to your friend about your guilt, but switch places with your friend and give yourself the advice they would probably give you.

4. Consider what your friend would think and say to you. They would likely say something like, "Hey, don't be so hard on yourself! We all make mistakes. I know you're still a good person."

5. Repeat whatever you think your dear friend would say, whether that's in your head, out loud, or down on paper. Say it a few times to let it sink in.

6. Think of how your friend would forgive you, and extend that same forgiveness to yourself.

THINK OF A LOVED ONE'S MISTAKE

While it's generally not a good idea to dwell on mistakes—your own or anyone else's—a little comparison can be a useful tool for improving your outlook. As humans, we all make mistakes, but we may find it difficult to remember this when we've recently made a big one. Remind yourself of a mistake one of your loved ones has made to help you work toward self-forgiveness.

Here's how to try this meditation:

1. Once you are prepared for your meditation session, think about a recent mistake you made. Don't dwell on it, but keep it in mind.
2. Now, think of a mistake that someone you love made. Try to find one that is comparable to your own. For example, if you messed up by losing your temper with your spouse, think about a time a friend lost their temper with their significant other.
3. Remind yourself of the consequences of that mistake. For example, your friend may have hurt their significant other's feelings or triggered an even bigger fight.
4. Think about how it was resolved. In the previous example, perhaps the couple ended up in counseling or had a good heart-to-heart about their relationship. Think about whether your feelings for your friend changed because of this instance (spoiler alert: they probably didn't).
5. Remind yourself that feelings about you (both your own feelings and others') don't need to change because of one mistake. Forgive yourself and commit to doing better next time.

PRACTICE LOVING–KINDNESS MEDITATION

If you haven't practiced loving-kindness meditation before, this exercise will be a great introduction. If you have, go ahead and give it another shot!

Loving-kindness meditation, or *metta bhavana*, is a type of meditation that focuses your energy and attention on kindness and friendliness toward yourself and others. It's a great way to become more self-compassionate and self-loving, making it significantly easier to extend forgiveness to yourself.

Here's how it works:

1. Think of several people close to you, people whom you love and cherish. Imagine them standing all around you, sending you their love and best wishes for your health and happiness. Bask in their love and positive vibes, soaking it all in.

2. Now switch it up by cultivating feelings of love and warmth for these people and sending these feelings their way. Repeat a few phrases designed to aid you in this endeavor, like:

   * May your life be filled with love and happiness.
   * May you know joy, peace, and satisfaction.
   * May you be free from pain and suffering.

3. Next, think of several people you feel neutral about (like your neighbors, colleagues, and other acquaintances), and send them the same good feelings.

4. In the final step, extend these same positive vibes and feelings of love to all living beings. Picture the world and send the love all around it.

CATALOG YOUR
LESSONS LEARNED

It's easier to forgive yourself when you can see the positives that can result from your mistakes. While it may feel like there's no upside to the mistakes you make, especially the big ones, that's virtually never true—even the gravest of errors can have positive outcomes. For example, you may have completely failed an interview because of overconfidence, but you can learn that there is a fine line between confidence and arrogance, and staying on the confidence side will serve you far better.

To catalog the lessons you learned from your mistakes, follow these steps:

1. Think about a recent mistake you made that had a noticeable impact on your life. It might be something that led to you getting passed over for a promotion, a breakup with your significant other, or a negative impact on your health.

2. Determine what the negative effects of this mistake were and how they are currently impacting you. Don't dwell on the negative side, but be aware of the consequences you've faced.

3. Think about what has changed in your life since then and what you have learned, gained, or grown from. For example, maybe the mistake that led to a breakup taught you about what you need in a relationship or helped you avoid settling for someone who wasn't right for you.

4. Write down the lesson(s) you learned. Identify how this mistake has changed your life so far and how it can positively impact you going forward.

CONFRONT YOUR INNER CRITIC

Sometimes you may feel that something external is holding you back from forgiving yourself and moving on, but you don't realize that it may be something far more insidious: your inner critic. We all have an inner critic that likes to pop up when we *least* need their opinion, but there are ways to combat this self-criticism! You can confront it and call its worldview into question, allowing you to be more forgiving and loving toward yourself.

This is how this meditation works:

1. After your meditation prep, sit quietly for a few minutes and observe your thoughts. It should be easy to catch your inner critic in action if you think about the mistakes you've made or the things you don't really love about yourself.
2. As soon as you catch your inner critic in action, stop it in its tracks. Listen to what it was saying, but don't immediately believe it.
3. Question the inner critic's premises. For example, if your inner critic says, "You're so stupid for making that mistake," think about whether that truly makes you stupid. Remind yourself that even the smartest people make mistakes, so perhaps making a mistake just makes you human rather than stupid.
4. Peel back the layers to see the faulty core belief(s) behind the criticism. For example, if the inner voice says, "Now you won't have any friends," note that the faulty belief is that you must be perfect to have friends. Clearly that's not true!

USE DEPERSONALIZATION
TO COPE WITH FAILURE

If you've heard of depersonalization before, you're probably wondering how in the world it can be used in a positive way. Generally, when people reference depersonalization, they are talking about a sense of detachment from yourself or your body, almost like watching yourself as another person. While this can be unhealthy if taken to an extreme, the basic concept can also be used in a healthy manner to help you cope with failure. Try the following meditation to figure out how.

1. When you're ready to begin, take a high-level perspective on yourself. Don't think about specific behaviors or quirks, just think about yourself as a whole person. Build a mental picture of yourself and leave some space around you, with a sort of "bubble" that marks your boundaries.

2. Bring to mind the failure that's been eating at you; however, instead of adding it to the mental picture of you, drop it just outside your bubble.

3. Think about your failure as something that occurred, but not something that makes you who you are. You are not your mistakes, and you don't need to rethink your whole identity when you make a mistake.

4. Look at yourself, smiling and happy in the bubble of "you" with your failure left out in the cold, and remind yourself that this is the reality.

MEDITATE ON COMMON HUMANITY

Have you ever spent time considering how you fit in with humanity as a whole? It might be an overwhelming idea, but it can help to ground yourself and build your sense of self-compassion. It never hurts to be reminded that you aren't alone in your struggles and that you have a lot in common with your fellow humans. Try this meditation to get in touch with your common humanity.

1. Think about humanity as a whole: There are about seven billion people on the planet right now. While you may know only a tiny percentage of those seven billion people, you probably don't think much about what you have in common with the rest of them. Imagine a vast sea of people, all unique, none of them exactly like the others.

2. Place yourself in the context of that sea of people. Think about what a complex being you are, with all your hopes, your dreams, your personality traits and quirks, your interests and likes and dislikes. Remind yourself that each and every person on the planet has their own complexities.

3. Although we are all unique, we all have something in common: our humanity. We are all living, breathing human beings who are struggling and succeeding and laughing and crying together. Meditate on this thought and allow yourself to feel a little bit less alone.

ALLOW YOURSELF
TO FEEL GUILTY

It sounds a little counterintuitive, but it's actually a helpful exercise in self-forgiveness to allow yourself to feel guilty. We tend to feel guilty when we've done something wrong, but we dislike feeling guilty, so we try to immediately deny, deflect, or assuage our guilt. Have you ever wondered what it would be like to simply accept your guilt, to allow yourself to feel guilty as a natural reaction to your mistakes? If you're struggling with guilt that just won't let go, try accepting it instead.

Here's how to do it:

1. Focus on your breathing and keep it steady and controlled while you pull up the guilt you've been feeling. Don't let it overwhelm you, but allow it to enter your consciousness and simply exist.

2. Sit with your guilt for a few minutes. Think about how it feels to sit with your guilt. It probably doesn't feel great, but that's okay—you know that life is not all sunshine and rainbows, and that you need to feel the rain sometimes.

3. Think about what guilt means and what its purpose is: Guilt means you have hurt someone, and its purpose is to discourage you from hurting people in the future. Accept that guilt has its place in your life and commit to letting it do its job.

4. Promise yourself to do better next time, thank your guilt for its contribution to your life, then set it aside and go on with your day.

VISUALIZE
FORGIVING YOURSELF

Visualizing yourself in a particular setting or engaging in an action is an effective way to make that scenario more believable and thus more achievable. To put the power of visualization to work for you in your quest for greater self-forgiveness, use the following guided meditation.

1. Breathe deeply and steadily, keeping yourself centered, then expand your awareness to include yourself. See yourself in your mind's eye.

2. Imagine what it would look like to forgive yourself. Visualize a carbon copy of yourself, standing in front of your original self.

3. Think about what you would say to apologize to yourself for a mistake that had a negative impact on you. It would probably sound similar to the apology you would give any loved one, but it will have the added weight of knowing exactly how the person on the receiving end was affected by your actions.

4. Decide exactly what you would say, and write it out if that helps you. Now, visualize delivering that apology to yourself. Have your "carbon copy" apologize to yourself.

5. Next, visualize yourself accepting the apology. Thank your carbon copy for the apology and accept it, then offer forgiveness. If it feels right, visualize a warm handshake or a hug to seal the deal!

WRITE OUT
AN APOLOGY

If you've ever written a letter of apology before, you know that it can be extremely cathartic. When you acknowledge what happened, admit your role in hurting someone, and ask for forgiveness, it can feel like a huge weight has been lifted off of you. Take advantage of the catharsis available to you and write out an apology letter, but address it to yourself.

1. Think about the mistakes you have made that resulted in you getting hurt, whether intentional or otherwise. Allow them into your consciousness slowly to avoid getting overwhelmed. Think about them in enough detail to know exactly where things went wrong. Note these mistakes in your journal or notebook.

2. Remove yourself from the role of victim and focus on your role as the perpetrator; however, remind yourself that you can make amends, since the victim is likely to hear you out!

3. Pour your heart out into an authentic, sincere letter of apology. Detail what you did, why it was wrong, and use the words "I'm sorry" or "I apologize."

4. Make sure to include all the mistakes you listed earlier and apologize for each one of them. This can take a while, but the resulting relief is worth it!

5. When you're finished, take off the "perpetrator" role and take on the "victim" role. Read the letter of apology and make the decision to accept it.

CULTIVATE PATIENCE
FOR YOURSELF

Patience is a virtue, as the old saying goes. Although we often reference this fact in relation to being patient with others, it's equally important to be patient with yourself. In fact, we are often the *most* impatient with ourselves! We know ourselves better than anyone, meaning we know exactly what our pitfalls and weaknesses are, but we should focus on using this knowledge to pick ourselves up rather than put ourselves down. To work on being more patient and forgiving toward yourself, use this patience meditation.

1. Begin by thinking about how long it takes to reach a big goal, like losing a significant amount of weight, going from a couch potato to a marathon runner, or building a successful business from scratch. Consider how much time you need to invest to achieve these goals—in some cases, it can be *years* before your goal is realized!

2. Remind yourself that becoming a more self-accepting, self-appreciating, and self-forgiving person is also a long-term goal. Think about how silly it would be to get impatient and frustrated with yourself for not being able to run a marathon a week after you began training for it.

3. Tell yourself that personal growth is a big goal, and you will not become your "goal self" overnight. Think about the value and the importance of patience and make a decision to prioritize being patient with yourself. Extend yourself a little love and go on with your day.

CHAPTER 5

MEDITATIONS ON BEING BODY POSITIVE

Modern society is notorious for telling us what's wrong with our bodies. Everywhere you look, there are advertisements and blogs and "influencers" telling you—directly or indirectly—that you need to fix your physical flaws in order to be loveable. With so many messages about the way you *should* look and how your value is dependent on your body weight, size, or shape, it's vital to combat the negativity with some body-positive thoughts. You can build a great amount of self-love and self-compassion simply through accepting your body as it is and embracing your flaws for what they are: things that make you "you." These meditations focus on identifying things you like about your body, accepting the things you don't like, practicing gratitude, relaxing and releasing tension, stretching, using visualization, and practicing the valuable skill of non-comparison, among others.

NAME THE THINGS
YOU LIKE

What do you like about your body? Although you may spend more time thinking about what you *don't* like about your body, there are sure to be at least a few things you do like about it. Use this exercise to identify those positive features.

Follow these steps:

1. After getting ready to meditate, take a few extra moments to really get into your physical self. Think about how it feels to be in your body and the sensations you notice. Take a few deep breaths and settle in.

2. Take a third-person perspective and look at your body. Use a compassionate and caring lens, as you are not looking for flaws. You are looking for positives!

3. Think about what you like about your body. Perhaps you have great calves, or strong shoulders. Maybe you like your eyes or your natural hair color. It could even be something small and seemingly unimportant, like the arch of your eyebrows or your belly button.

4. Think of at least five things you like about your body and write them down in a journal or notebook. Include details and descriptors, like "I like my strong, muscular calves" or "I like my piercing, sea-green eyes."

5. Look back over your list and use it to remind yourself that there are some really great things about your body.

IDENTIFY YOUR BEST FEATURE

This meditation is similar to the previous one, Name the Things You Like, but it's more focused and will pull input from other people. It's best to work on getting your self-confidence from yourself and finding validation within, but there's nothing wrong with getting a boost from others once in a while. Give this meditation a try to figure out what your best feature is, and work on appreciating it more.

Follow these steps:

1. Once you're prepared to meditate, keep your eyes closed and continue to breathe regularly. Turn your attention toward your memories, and begin to search them.

2. You're searching your memories to find instances where people in your life gave you a compliment or noted a positive physical feature. Hopefully you remember quite a few, as people generally give us more compliments than we realize!

3. When you have identified a few compliments, look to see if you can find a pattern. Are most of them about how pretty your eyes are? Or perhaps they're about your toned arms, or the shape of your nose.

4. Consider whether you agree that this is your best feature, and if not, compare it to your personal favorite feature. Whichever one wins out, let yourself feel some pride and pleasure in your best physical feature.

SHOW YOUR
BODY GRATITUDE

This meditation is a great way to boost your acceptance of and compassion for yourself. Both body positivity and gratitude are also excellent goals in and of themselves! We often view our bodies with an eye for flaws and a cynical perspective, but that's not conducive to a healthy relationship with yourself and your body. Instead, start practicing gratitude for your own body.

Follow these steps to give it a try:

1. At the tail end of your meditation preparation, bring the focus to your body. Be attentive to how it feels and how you feel about it. Notice whether you're holding on to any physical tension or negative thoughts toward your body.

2. Set aside any discomfort or criticisms you have about your body, and replace them with gratitude.

3. To cultivate a sense of gratitude, start at your heart. Gather up all the warm, friendly, and loving feelings within yourself and hold onto them. Let them grow and expand as you find more warmth and love within yourself.

4. Once you feel you've gathered up all the good vibes you can, send them out into your body. Feel the warmth traveling through you. Give your body your sincere thanks for all it does for you.

ACCEPT YOUR BODY AS IT IS

One of the keys to feeling compassion and love for your body is to first accept it exactly as it is. If you can't accept the reality of your body, then any love you cultivate for it will be based on a faulty perspective. To ensure you end up with true, unadulterated love and compassion for your body, start by working on accepting it exactly as it is.

1. After getting set up for your meditation session, sit with your body for a while. Settle in and get comfortable with being in your body.
2. Zoom out and, using a third-person perspective, take a look at your body. See it as it really is, with its unique features, strengths, weaknesses, warts, stray hairs, and all.
3. Your body may not look or feel exactly as you want it to, but it is yours. It's the only body you have, and it has gotten you to this point in life!
4. Turn your attention to function. Think about what your body allows you to do. Again, your body might not be able to do everything you'd like, but it carries you through your days.
5. With both form and function in mind, focus on accepting your body as it is. It might be easier to think about what you'd like to improve, but for this exercise channel all of your energy into accepting your body exactly as it is, without caveat.

ACCEPT YOUR BODY AS IT WILL BE

This meditation can be helpful for anyone, but it will be especially helpful for those going through a big change, like pregnancy or a serious health issue. Instead of accepting your body as it is now and leaving it there, work on accepting your body as it *will be*. This is how you develop true, lasting acceptance of your body.

Here's what you do:

1. As you prepare for your meditation session, spend a little extra time on getting centered and grounded in your own body. Feel what it's like to be in your body and notice the sensations that come with it.

2. When you feel completely "in" your body, think about the impending change. We'll use pregnancy as an example that many people can identify with. Imagine what your pregnancy will feel like as it progresses.

3. Think about the physical changes you will undergo. There are many changes that can happen, but think about the most likely ones, including stretch marks on a rapidly expanding belly, fuller breasts, and even swollen calves and ankles.

4. Remind yourself that these changes are normal, natural, and symptoms that accompany a beautiful part of being human. Accept that all of these changes will most likely happen to your body, and they will not change your worth as a person.

EMBRACE AGING

This meditation can be especially effective for people who are feeling the effects of aging or worried about them in the future. Although accepting your body as it is now will have some excellent benefits, even more significant benefits can be gleaned from learning to accept your body as it ages. To give it a shot, try these steps:

1. Once you are prepared for meditation, turn your attention to your body. Sit in it, live in it, and get a sense of exactly what it feels like to be in your body. Spend a few moments here.

2. When you feel grounded and fully within your own body, cast forward with your mind's eye and think about your body at a point in the future. At the point in time that you choose, think about what your life will be like. Think about what you will have accomplished and the love that will permeate your life.

3. Now focus your mind on your body. Think about what it will look like; it will probably have some wrinkles, some gray hairs, and some looser skin than it has now. You may have crow's feet and smile lines too.

4. Instead of dwelling on these changes and attributing negative judgments to them, think about what they actually are: signs of a long life, full of wisdom and joy and opportunity. Accept that your body will eventually look very different than it does now, and that's okay.

BRAINSTORM
SOME POSSIBILITIES

If you struggle with accepting your body as it is because there are so many changes you'd like to make, this meditation can help you straddle the line between self-acceptance and self-improvement. It's okay to be dissatisfied with parts of yourself, but remember to temper your self-criticism with a healthy dose of self-compassion; you can work toward a solution by considering what you can do to alleviate or reverse any dissatisfaction you feel about your body.

Here's one way to do that:

1. Grab your journal and something to write with before you start prepping for meditation. Proceed through your normal meditation prep as usual.

2. Now, turn your attention to your body and what you'd like to change about it. If a couple of negative thoughts come up, allow them to exist in your mind but let them go as quickly as they came.

3. Write down each of your areas in which you desire change and leave room to write in between them. For example, you might write "weak arms" or "flaky, dry skin."

4. Under each area, brainstorm some possibilities for positive change. These can be both for improving the area and for accepting it as it is. For example, you could write "lifting weights" to improve your arms, but also "give myself hugs." Both will help you accept and love your body as it is, and encourage you to take care of it. Continue to brainstorm possibilities for each of your "problem" areas and refer back to the list when you are inspired to make a positive change.

MEDITATE TO RELEASE TENSION

Tension is not necessarily a bad thing, but too much of it too often can have a negative impact on you and your health, both mental and physical. It's common to build up tension in your muscles when you are feeling stressed or dealing with challenging situations. To help you take care of your body and your mind, try this meditation to release the tension you've been holding on to.

1. After your usual meditation prep, take another deep, slow inhale, hold it for a couple moments, then slowly exhale it fully out of your nose. Repeat this deep breath until you feel your heartbeat matches your breath.

2. Turn your attention to your body. Feel where you are holding tension. Is it in your shoulders? Your neck? Perhaps your lower back? You might even store it in your buttocks or in your hamstrings. Wherever your tension resides, find it and take note of it.

3. Now, focus your attention on one area at a time. Pour your energy into this area, letting your calmness wash over it and carry away the tension. Continue this practice with each area where you are holding on to tension.

4. Once you finish the practice in your last area, go back to the first and check in—is it still relaxed and tension-free? If not, go for a second round of releasing tension.

5. Continue until your whole body is more relaxed and you can breathe a little easier.

WAKE UP
YOUR BODY

Sometimes the way to feel a little bit better about yourself and your body is to get it going! In today's world, we spend a lot of time sitting, lying down, and generally not moving much. To break up the sedentary routine, try a meditation to wake up your body.

Follow these instructions to give it a shot:

1. As you finish your meditation preparations, turn your attention to your body. Note how it feels right now, whether you have any aches and pains or feel particularly tired or strained in any area.

2. Start gathering your energy and visualize putting it into a little ball. If you're having trouble finding the energy, think about getting it from the sun, the air around you, or the food you've eaten today. Search out anywhere you can pull energy from and use it.

3. Continue gathering energy until you can feel it pulsing in your hands, then send it throughout your body.

4. Visualize the energy moving from the imaginary ball to your hands, your arms, up to your head and neck, and down all the way to your toes. As it travels, feel it move through your body. As it reaches your shoulders, give them a little squeeze. Flex your thighs when it reaches them, then squeeze your calves as it travels through them.

5. Allow the energy to move through your entire body, waking it up and breathing life into it.

STRETCH MINDFULLY

If you've ever taken a gym class in school, you know that stretching is an important part of staying fit and healthy. But how often do you actually stretch? Further, how often do you stretch *mindfully*, with the express purpose of refreshing and rejuvenating your body? If you're like most of us, probably not often enough! Use this exercise to give your body the stretches it needs to stay healthy and taken care of.

1. In your comfortable seated position, keep your eyes closed but lift your arms over your head. Reach for the sky, lengthening your spine while keeping your shoulders away from your ears. Feel the sensations in your arms and your back as your muscles move to accommodate your stretch.

2. Next, push your hands out in front of you, interlacing your fingers with your palms facing out. Hold this stretch for a few moments. Notice how it feels to round your back and push away from you.

3. Now take your hands and join them behind you, interlacing your fingers again. Press out and up with your palms facing away from your body. Notice the tightness between your shoulder blades.

4. Return to your resting position and note how you feel now. Hopefully, you feel a little more relaxed and comfortable!

LEARN TO LOVE
YOUR FLAWS

It's a tall order, but learning to love your flaws is a surefire way to boost your love and acceptance for yourself and build your self-compassion. You don't need to accept and embrace behaviors that make you unhealthy (e.g., smoking or binge eating), but you can benefit greatly from learning to accept and love yourself as you are, flaws and all.

1. Grab a journal or a notebook for this exercise, then begin your meditation as you usually do. Give yourself some extra love and affection to prepare yourself.
2. Next, think about your physical flaws or features you dislike. What do you wish you could change about yourself? Do you think your nose is too big, your fingers too chubby, your legs too lanky? Whatever your perceived flaws are, write them down.
3. Look over your list and make note of which flaws limit your life in some way. Does your nose keep you from fitting through doorways? Do your chubby fingers prohibit you from typing? Are your legs so long that you can't support your weight?
4. You will probably find that your flaws do not, in fact, limit your life. Instead of focusing on the flaws that don't actually inhibit you, know that your limitations are self-imposed and all in your head.
5. Think of these flaws as features that make you unique rather than as insurmountable obstacles. Give each of these flaws some love, as they make you who you are.

MEDITATE ON WHAT IT MEANS TO YOU TO BE HEALTHY

We hear the word "healthy" used a lot. In fact, it's used dozens of times in this book alone, and this book is not even focused directly on health! There are lots of thoughts on what makes a person healthy and what doesn't, but at the end of the day it's simply not that important what other people think about being healthy—what matters is what *you* think of as healthy. To work on feeling healthy and happy in your own body, try this meditation:

1. Focus on your body. Think about how it feels to be in your body. Does it generally feel good or do you struggle?

2. If you struggle sometimes, don't worry! We all do. Instead of dwelling on it, ask yourself these questions:

    * Do you feel healthy and happy with yourself?
    * Do you have the energy to do what you want to do?
    * Are you comfortable simply being in your body?

3. Now, consider what it would take to feel healthy and happy with yourself, how much energy you need to do what you want to do, and what it would take to feel comfortable in your own body.

4. Take your answers to these questions and use them as the basis for your personal definition of what it means to be healthy.

PRACTICE
NON-COMPARISON

When we avoid comparing ourselves to others and accept and love our bodies for what they are, we are at our happiest and healthiest; however, it's one of those things that's easy to identify as a misstep, but hard to actually stop doing. The media's constant focus on attractiveness and beauty certainly doesn't help you in this endeavor, but you have more power than you think. Try this guided meditation to work on cutting the comparisons with two salient points.

1. First, think about what it means to compare yourself to others. You might not think of it this way immediately, but comparing yourself to others is usually done with the intent to judge one "better" and one "worse," or one "superior" and one "inferior." Either way your judgment lands, you're only raising one up at the expense of the other.

2. Remind yourself that thinking of others in a negative light doesn't lift you up any higher, it just pushes others down (and often yourself as well, even if you don't realize it).

3. Next, think about how useful comparisons really are. Does your happiness depend on being better or worse than the next person? Will feeling momentarily better about yourself as a result of comparison actually build lasting happiness? You will likely conclude that these comparisons are not actually effective.

4. With these two points in mind (that comparisons are inherently flawed and also ineffective), commit to boosting yourself up without putting others down.

VISUALIZE BODY POSITIVITY AS NOURISHMENT FOR THE HEART

When you engage in self-care and self-development, it's vital that you see your efforts actually resulting in positive outcomes. Whether those outcomes are simple relaxation, a slightly more positive mood, or a more well-rounded and confident self, we like to know that our actions will benefit us. To show yourself how body positivity and self-compassion can help you, try visualizing body positivity as nourishment for your heart. Here's how to do it:

1. See yourself practicing body positivity. If you need some concrete examples, try one of the other meditations in this chapter first, then come back to this one.
2. Watch as you engage in the meditation, and imagine that a visible substance is produced. Visualize it however works best for you, but you can use this one if you can't think of anything: a smooth, flowing, plasma-like substance in a pretty color. See it being created as you engage in body positivity and watch as it gathers above your head.
3. As you watch yourself finishing the meditation, "see" this substance hang in the air above you, gently rippling with positivity. Now visualize it being slowly reabsorbed into your body, bringing with it all the good feelings you just produced and more.
4. Follow the substance as it seeps into you, traveling to your heart and strengthening it. Watch as it makes you stronger, more resilient, and more compassionate.

DISREGARD
THE NEGATIVE

It's a wise practice to approach others for advice and ideas, and it's wonderful to allow yourself to be built up and encouraged by the kind people in your life; however, relying on others for your self-love is a double-edged sword. If you get your validation from others, then what do you do when you receive negative comments? To mitigate the potential damage that negative comments can bring without closing yourself off to others, practice disregarding the negative.

1. Think about how it feels to receive negative comments about your body; if you can't think of any, imagine how it feels to get such comments.
2. Consider whether these comments were made in love or out of some other motive or emotion. Separate the constructive from the just-plain-mean comments.
3. Imagine these negative comments being sent toward you. Visualize yourself in the center, with the comments flying at you.
4. Instead of letting them hit you, visualize a barrier around you. When the negative remarks hit the barrier, they fall to the floor, completely harmless. Continue this visualization for a couple minutes and watch as they all fail to hit the target.
5. These comments symbolize negativity about your body, and the barrier symbolizes your decision to disregard them completely. Dedicate yourself to keeping up this barrier and protecting yourself from any unnecessary negativity about your body. Decide to love yourself no matter what anyone else tells you.

CHAPTER 6

MEDITATIONS ON ACCEPTING LOVE

Your ability to accept love is at the heart of your capacity for self-compassion. After all, if you struggle to accept love from any source, how are you supposed to give yourself the love you need? At its core, self-compassion is all about accepting and loving yourself as you are—even if you still want to improve or change some of your less desirable qualities—which requires you to be able to accept love. The meditations in this chapter are all about learning to accept love from others, from yourself, and even from your pets! They will help you practice accepting love using a variety of techniques, including receiving compliments, being open to the warmth of others, using affirmations to assert your worthiness to accept love, identifying your hang-ups, and using visualization to make it easier and more comfortable to accept love from others.

GIVE YOURSELF PERMISSION TO ACCEPT LOVE

The first step in opening yourself up to accepting love from other people is to give yourself permission to do so. You can try all the techniques in the world, but if you haven't given yourself the okay to accept love, you will always have a block. First work on opening yourself up to the possibility, then you can move on to trying different exercises to help you put it into practice.

Here's how to give yourself permission:

1. Prepare for meditation as you usually do, but spend a little extra time on each step. Be slow and deliberate, and gentle with yourself.

2. Once you're ready, think about your natural ability to accept love. Figure out where the line is for you; is it easy to accept love from family but not from friends? Or perhaps you can accept small shows of affection, but not the more serious displays of love.

3. Wherever the line is, visualize pushing it just a bit further out. Give yourself permission to accept more love from everyone in your life. Tell yourself that there's nothing wrong with accepting love, and that it is a gift to others when you receive their love.

4. Continue to push that line just a little further every time you meditate, and soon you will find that you can accept any show of love that is directed toward you.

ACCEPT
A COMPLIMENT

If you have trouble accepting compliments, you're not alone! Many of us have trouble accepting the nice things that our friends and family say to us. It's odd that we can have so much trouble simply accepting the kind, loving comments from people we know and trust, but it's a common phenomenon. Luckily, there's hope for those of you in this situation! You can train yourself to get better at receiving warmth and kindness from others.

To get started, try this meditation:

1. Sit quietly for a little while after prepping for your meditation. Focus your attention on the love in your life. Think about those you love most, and those who love you most.
2. Get yourself in a positive mindset by wrapping yourself in their warmth and affection. Open yourself up to receiving all the good that your loved ones have to offer.
3. Think about a recent compliment someone gave you. Pick someone close to you, since the closer they are, the more meaningful the compliments tend to be.
4. Repeat the compliment in your head a few times, and see how it feels. If it still feels unnatural or uncomfortable, remind yourself that your loved one genuinely cares about you and would want you to accept the compliment fully.

Revisit this process periodically and/or whenever you get a compliment that you find difficult to accept.

GET
A HUG

Getting a hug seems like a pretty easy thing to do, but there is a caveat: You can't just get a hug; you need to be fully open to receiving the hug and everything it represents. If you hug infrequently or often find it difficult to engage in a prolonged hug, this is the meditation for you! It will help you learn how to accept this loving physical act of affection.

Follow these steps to work a hug into your meditation:

1. Instead of preparing for meditation as you usually do, check in with someone you love and ask if they would like to take part in an important meditation exercise.
2. Once you find your hugging partner, prep for your meditation either alone or with them. Walk them through how to meditate if they don't already know. (Tip: You can direct them to the Preparing to Meditate section at the beginning of the book.)
3. Once you're prepped and you're both ready, incorporate the hug. Come together in a warm embrace. Put your head to the right of their head, which aligns your heart with theirs when you hug.
4. Breathe deeply as you hug, keeping your mind calm and free of thoughts of shame, judgment, or discomfort. Simply enjoy the feeling of being hugged. Bonus points if you align your breath with theirs as well!
5. Stay for a few moments, then thank them and break apart with warmth and affection for one another.

PRACTICE ACCEPTING WARMTH FROM OTHERS

Although this exercise is similar to a previous one in this chapter (Accept a Compliment), it isn't quite as restrictive. People show warmth in many ways, whether that's through compliments, a hug, or a matter-of-fact statement on their feelings about someone. For a couple of days, pay attention to the ways people in your life show you love.

1. When you're ready to begin, go through your meditation prep with a focus on emanating warmth and being open to feeling warmth from others.
2. Next, call to mind a few examples of the people in your life showing you love and affection. It can help to write down these examples so that you can go into detail in your head.
3. Keep your heart open as you relive these experiences. Write down what happened and how it felt to be the recipient of such warmth from others. Remind yourself to purposefully reach out for the glowing feelings you experienced when it first happened.
4. Visualize that warmth as a ball of light that's warm in color. This can be whatever color makes sense to you, but if you're not sure, you can go with a warm, orangey yellow.
5. Imagine that ball of light traveling from your loved one's hand to yours and soaking into your body. See it suffuse you with warmth and love.
6. Focus on how it feels to receive this warmth from others. Bask in it and remind yourself that it's okay to receive love.

RELIVE GETTING A GREAT GIFT

Have you ever gotten a gift so great or so perfect for you that you felt like a kid on Christmas morning? If so, you know what a mood-booster that can be! It can also help you become more open to receiving from others since it's such a positive experience. To use your gift-receiving memory as a tool to boost your receptivity, try the following steps:

1. Continue to sit quietly after your meditation prep and turn your focus to your memories. Search them for the best gift(s) you've ever received. Think back all the way to your childhood if you need to.
2. Once you've selected the memory, spend a few moments sinking into it. Try to remember all the details about this memory: what the occasion was, what you were doing before you got the gift, your reaction to it, even the smells and sounds surrounding you at the time. Relive it as realistically as possible.
3. Think about how it felt to receive that gift. Consider the care that your gift-giver put into picking out and delivering your gift, and what that says about their love for you.
4. Savor those warm, fuzzy feelings and remember that the only way to get more of them is to open yourself up to receiving from others. Commit to doing exactly that!

MAKE A LIST OF PEOPLE
WHO LOVE YOU

This meditation is a great way to remind yourself of the capacity for love and care in your life. If you ever need a little boost of love to get your own self-love going, the outcome of this meditation will give you an excellent tool to do just that!

Here's how to do it:

1. Get your journal or a notebook out and something to write with, then proceed with the usual meditation prep. When you're ready, sit for a few moments and focus your attention on love.

2. Think about the people in your life who show you they love you. Keep in mind there are several different ways to show love. It might help to list some ways people show love (for help with this, check out List Your Favorite Ways to Show Love in Chapter 7), then think about who shows you love through each method.

3. Write out your list. Try to include as many people as possible. If you're not totally sure about someone's feelings toward you, assume that there is some love there.

4. Envision all of these people who love you and visualize all the love they have for you. Let it in, soak it all up, and allow it to lift your mood and encourage your own self-love. You can refer back to the list whenever you need a boost!

LIST YOUR FAVORITE WAYS TO RECEIVE LOVE

There are so many ways to receive love that listing them all here would take up the entire book! Instead of simply listing the ways to receive love, this exercise will walk you through determining your personal favorites. When you identify how you want to receive love, it makes you more open to receiving love in these ways. Give it a try by following these steps:

1. Continue breathing deeply and getting centered in your practice. Next, turn your attention to love.

2. Think about the ways you have received love in your life. If it helps, you can write them down. For help getting started, here are a few common ways to receive love: receiving hugs and other physical displays of affection, being the recipient of acts of service, and accepting gifts and/or compliments.

3. Once you have a list of at least five to ten ways you have received love in your life, try to narrow it down to your top two or three.

4. Think about what has made you happiest or most engaged with the giver. If you call to mind the best moments, do you find a pattern? For example, maybe all of them involve physical touch or cuddling.

5. When you have your favorite ways identified, commit to being more open to receiving love in these ways. This will help you receive even more love from your everyday interactions with loved ones.

VISUALIZE OPENING YOUR HEART

Visualization is a powerful tool for opening yourself up to the good in life (and for sending out good things to others). If you haven't tried it yet, you're in for a treat! This meditation will walk you through a visualization intended to help you open yourself up to receiving love from others. Approach it with an open and willing mind, and an open and willing heart is sure to follow!

1. Focus your internal gaze on your heart when you are relaxed and ready to meditate. Send all of your energy here until you can see it pulsing.

2. Now, visualize your heart opening up. See your heart as something that is even better when it's open, like a flower bud with petals unfolding, rather than an actual human heart—you don't want it literally opening up!

3. Watch as it unfolds. Know that, although it is more vulnerable this way, it is also open to receiving real love. Tell yourself that the trade-off is worth it, because it truly is. It's true that it's better to have loved and lost it than to have never loved at all; every experience of love helps you grow and become a better person.

4. Visualize holding your heart open like this for at least a few minutes. Try to keep your heart open as you come out of your meditative state and go on with your day.

IDENTIFY YOUR OBSTACLES TO ACCEPTING LOVE

Sometimes we have obstacles that get in between us and receiving love from others, despite our most sincere intention to be able to accept love. If there seems to be something holding you back from accepting love, you might have some obstacles you need to identify. Use this meditation to figure out what is in your way, then you can begin to address it.

1. Think about how it feels to accept love from the important people in your life: You get the nice warm, fuzzy feelings; you have a sense that you are understood and cared for. It feels great to be on the receiving end of love!

2. Now consider what stops you from receiving love. How does it make you feel when you try to accept affection and kindness from others? Search your feelings to find the culprit. You might realize that you feel as though you are not worthy of their love, for example.

3. Whatever you identify, write it down in a journal or notebook. Make a list of the reasons that you find. Next, think about how to address each of these obstacles to accepting love. For instance, if you don't feel worthy of receiving love, you would note that you are struggling with low self-esteem and might decide to visit a therapist to help you deal with it. Make sure you have an idea for how to address each reason before you finish the session.

CONCENTRATE ON YOUR LOVE FOR ONE PERSON

If the idea of opening yourself up to receiving love from everyone in your life is simply too big and abstract for you to manage, you can try biting off a smaller piece. It's a common tactic whenever you have a big project or goal in mind: Split it up into smaller tasks and start with a baby step. In this case, the baby step is focusing on your love for one person and using that to open yourself up to receiving love from more directions.

1. Expand your awareness from yourself to a person of your choosing. This person should be someone you have a lot of love for, and whom you want to show that love for. You might consider choosing your spouse, your child, your parent, or your dearest friend.

2. Meditate on your love for this person. Think about how it feels to love them, and how it feels to indulge in your love for them and show them affection. Sit with your love for a minute or two, enjoying the feeling.

3. Now, think about how it feels for this person when you share your love with them. Imagine what goes through their head, and how happy it makes them that someone loves them so completely.

4. Use this idea—your loved one reveling in your love—to remind yourself that receiving love is a wonderful part of the human experience, and it should be for you as well.

USE AFFIRMATIONS TO HELP YOU ACCEPT LOVE

If you haven't used affirmations before, you're about to learn a really helpful tool for a variety of goals! Affirmations are simple sentences that you repeat to yourself at least once a day. They help you stay focused on your goals, contribute to your overall self-image, and improve your outlook on whatever issue or topic you are focusing on. Use the following guide to develop and use affirmations for accepting love.

1. Think about how it feels to accept love from those dearest to you. Feel the emotions that arise when you imagine getting a loving hug or kind words from a loved one. Remind yourself how great it is to be loved! Set an intention to be more open to this love from others using affirmations.

2. Create your affirmations using these three guidelines:
   * They must be from the first-person perspective (e.g., use "I").
   * They must be in the present tense (e.g., "I am..." not "I will be...").
   * They must be positive and uplifting (e.g., "I am..." not "I am not...").

3. These affirmations can be focused on anything that you think will help you to receive love. Some example affirmations include:
   * "I am a good person who is worthy of receiving love."
   * "I am open to receiving love."
   * "I deserve to receive love from the important people in my life."

VISUALIZE A LOVE BANK

You might be wondering what a "love bank" is. It sounds like it could describe a lot of things—some of them only appropriate for adults— but for the purposes of this meditation, a love bank is a term used for what you visualize; you could also think of it as an "affection jar" or a "care package" or any other term that suits. Follow these steps to find out what a love bank is and how it can help you:

1. When you're ready, turn your focus to your inner, authentic self. Think about how it makes you feel when you receive love from others; does it make your inner self sing?
2. Think about how great it would be to create an inner store of love and draw from it whenever you need a boost. Instead of appreciating the love you receive and moving on, you could deposit it into your internal bank and withdraw it later as needed.
3. Visualize what your internal bank would look like. See it in detail: the storefront, the sign on top, the windows, and so on. Now see yourself going into the bank with the latest display of affection you have received, and watch yourself deposit it. Feel your heart swell a bit with the extra love.
4. For the next day, practice depositing all the love you receive, and pull a little of it out at the end of the day. Revel in the feeling of being loved!

FLIP YOUR PERSPECTIVE

Sometimes just changing how you look at things can have a huge impact on how you approach and experience them. Receiving love from others is one area in which your perspective is vital in determining how well the experience unfolds for you. To make it easier to receive the care and affection of others, try flipping your perspective.

1. Expand your awareness from yourself to others in your life. Think about the people closest to you and call up the love you feel for them. Consider how you like to show them your love, whether it's through kind words, thoughtful gifts, or warm hugs.

2. Now, imagine that none of these people were open to receiving your love anymore. If you shared kind words with them, they would brush them off or disagree. If you gave them a thoughtful gift, they would hand it back. If you tried to hug them, they would back away or simply refuse to hug you back. This would really hurt, wouldn't it?

3. Tell yourself that that's what you are doing when you refuse to receive love from others. Like you, the people in your life love to share their affection for you and show you they care. Remind yourself that receiving love is not a one-sided act, but one that requires acceptance on both sides and benefits both sides equally.

4. Set an intention to be more open to receiving love in the future.

MEDITATE
WITH A PET

If you had to pick one person who loves you unconditionally, who is always happy to see you, and who loves to get whatever physical attention you're willing to give, who would it be? Trick question—it's not a person, it's obviously your pet! There's nothing like the affections of a furry friend to encourage you to accept love. If you don't have a pet at home, see if you can borrow a friend or family member's pet to meditate with. Here's how to include your pet pal:

1. Before you prepare for your session, make sure your pet is nearby. If your pet is a lap warmer, get him or her settled on your lap before you begin. Next, go through your usual preparation.

2. With your pet at hand, turn your attention toward them. Stroke their fur slowly and gently, feeling every sensation. Note how soft and fluffy they are, or how smooth, or how wiry their hair is.

3. Open your eyes and look at your pet. Study their face and notice the details, like the color of their eyes, their eyelashes, and the hairs around their nose. When you look into their eyes, open yourself up to the love that they have for you. You should be able to see it easily reflected back at you!

4. Enjoy the feeling of being loved so deeply and so fiercely, and use the good feeling to encourage yourself to be open to receiving love from other sources.

PRACTICE ASKING FOR KINDNESS WHEN YOU NEED IT

We're humans, and it's a fact that sometimes we need a little bit of kindness from others. Even the most cheerful and upbeat among us need a little extra love once in a while, and we may occasionally find it difficult to ask for what we need. Use this meditation to help you practice asking for a little kindness from your loved ones when you need it.

1. When you're ready, think about a time recently when you needed a little boost. Maybe you got some bad news, you had an unlucky day, or you were just in a bad mood. Remember what it felt like to be in your shoes in that moment.

2. Now think about what would have helped you. Perhaps a friend could have delivered a coffee or met you for lunch to cheer you up. Or maybe all you really needed was to hear some words of affirmation from your partner. Think about how simple these things are and how willing you would be to do them for someone you love.

3. Imagine if you had reached out and asked for some kindness. How would that have influenced your mood? Would it have given you the boost you needed?

4. Commit to being more willing to ask for some kindness when you need it. Know that you are not weak when you ask for help—it actually takes a lot of inner strength to reach out when you're feeling down!

CHAPTER 7

MEDITATIONS ON GIVING LOVE

Giving love is one of the best things you can do in this life. It feels good, it's easy to do, and it makes both your life and the lives of those you love better; however, sometimes it can be a challenge to open yourself up and give that love to others. If you've been hurt or you're struggling to love yourself first, it's not such a simple thing to share your love for others; but the good news is that it can be done! This chapter contains several techniques you can use to practice sharing your love with others, including visualizing it, focusing on one loved one at a time, and thinking about the best ways to give and receive love.

GIVE YOURSELF PERMISSION TO LOVE

Like many other techniques in this book, the first step in actually applying it is to give yourself permission to use it. You can go through the motions all day long, but if your heart isn't really in it (because your head doesn't allow it), you're not going to get anywhere. If you find it difficult to allow yourself to give love to others, give this meditation a try.

1. Continue breathing deeply, inhaling through your nose and exhaling through your nose. Wrap yourself in a big hug, give yourself a squeeze, then return to your resting position.

2. Think about how it feels to give your love to others. When you have given your love to others in the past, how did it feel? Did it drain you or invigorate you? Unless you were in a toxic relationship, giving love probably felt great!

3. Remember what that feels like, and hang on to that memory. Remind yourself of it whenever you feel unable or unwilling to share your love with others.

4. Commit to experiencing more of this feeling in the future by giving yourself permission to love. It might help to visualize yourself actually giving the permission you need, and accepting that permission. Open your heart up to give love, and you will find that your capacity for love (toward others and yourself) is greatly expanded.

VISUALIZE GIVING A LOVED ONE A GIFT

There's not much that beats the feeling of getting a great gift from someone who knows and loves you! Not only is the gift great in and of itself, it's also a tangible reminder of the lengths our loved ones will go to in order to show us what we mean to them. Even if it's a small or inexpensive gift, it can still be incredibly meaningful. To nurture your compassion and love for others, use the idea of gift-giving as a meditation tool.

1. Think about one of the people you love the most, and think about what they would appreciate receiving. Maybe your wife would love to have tickets to her favorite band's concert, or your musician friend would jump for joy to receive a new instrument. Don't worry so much about the cost, just focus on what your loved one would appreciate.

2. Imagine that you pulled it off—you got them this perfect gift! Think about how excited you would feel in the days, hours, and moments leading up to the gift's unveiling.

3. Now, visualize actually giving your loved one this gift. See how their face would light up, how their eyes might fill with tears, and how big their smile would be.

4. Imagine how it would feel to be the instigator of this great joy. Hold on to this warm, happy feeling, and remind yourself that you can experience it by giving others joy whenever you can.

SEND OUT
FUZZY FEELINGS

Don't you just adore the warm, fuzzy feelings you get from spending time with people you love? Fuzzy feelings make your chest feel warm, soften your heart, and bring you a wonderful sense of contentment. You might not have felt these feelings in a while. If not, that's okay—we're going to cultivate them with this meditation!

1. First, bring up some of these fuzzy feelings. If you have a significant other, a child, or another person that is near and dear to you, bring them to mind. Think about some of your best moments with this person, moments in which you felt peace and joy and love during your time with them.

2. Gather these feelings and visualize holding them in your hands. Next, take your hands and grab onto the edges of these feelings, then start slowly moving your hands apart. Stretch them like you would stretch play dough, but imagine that they don't lose any volume; they simply multiply as they expand!

3. Now that you have a big mass of fuzzy feelings, visualize sending them out in every direction. Guide them toward the people you want to receive them. This can be anyone from your immediate family to your friends to your coworkers, or even people you've never met. Send out these fuzzy feelings like you can't wait to share them, and attach a prayer or wish to them with the hope of your recipients receiving them wholeheartedly.

FOCUS ON
LOVING ONE PERSON

Sometimes you need to start small with your self-development, and that's okay—you don't need to get anywhere overnight! As long as you are making small, positive steps, you are moving in the right direction. If you struggle with giving love to those around you, it's fine to start with giving your love to one person, and this meditation will help you do just that.

1. Call to mind the one person you care about the most in the world. It's okay if you have a tie for first place, just pick one of them!

2. Visualize this person in your head. See them smiling, laughing, and waving at you. Notice how it feels when they send this positive energy your way. You can likely feel it in your chest, like a tightening and relaxing sensation all at once. You might notice that it makes you smile and softens your forehead and your eyes too.

3. Think about how wonderful it is to receive love from him or her, and how wonderful it is to return it. Remind yourself that you can get a similar wonderful feeling from sharing your affections with the other people in your life.

4. You don't need to send it out right now, but start to get comfortable with the idea of sending these loving feelings to other people too.

VISUALIZE
SENDING YOUR LOVE

A great way to use visualization is to imagine showing your love for the people you care for most. It can feel a bit abstract to "send your love" to someone without taking the time to build it, package it, and send it on its way. To make it more concrete, practice visualizing this loving act.

Here's how to do it:

1. Start by visualizing your love for the people who are dearest to you. Think about what it looks like. Is it a ball with smooth edges? A disorganized mass of good thoughts? A big box chock-full of affection? Whatever it is, focus on this image. See it in as much detail as possible, including color, shape, texture, size, patterns, and so on.

2. Once you have a good idea what it looks like, think about how you can send it out. Do you need little gift boxes or can you send it as is? Visualize packaging up your love into personalized deliveries for those you love most, and gather them all together.

3. Now, all at once, send out the packages. See yourself dropping them in a big mailbox or sending them out on little wings, headed straight to your loved ones.

4. Watch as all these positive, fuzzy feelings make their way out and toward the people you love, and allow yourself a satisfied smile.

MAKE A LIST OF PEOPLE YOU LOVE

Sometimes all you need to remind you of the love you have to give and your capacity for giving is a good list! This meditation is especially fun for gleeful list-makers (like the author of this book), but it can benefit anyone who wants to work on being more loving and giving, both for others and for themselves.

1. Before you proceed with your meditation prep, make sure you have a notebook or pad of paper handy, then prepare for the meditation.

2. When you're ready, pull out a pen and get ready to write. Think about all the people who love you. It can be helpful to start with the obvious ones, like family and dear friends.

3. Write them down, but don't limit yourself to family and friends. Be liberal with your definition of love and include anyone whom you show affection or care for. This can include co-workers, friends of friends, or even the barista who makes your morning coffee.

4. Look at your list and imagine how much love that adds up to. Allow yourself to feel grateful for all the love you get to give in your life, and say a quick prayer or gratitude mantra to acknowledge the great amount of love you have to give. Refer back to this list whenever you are feeling short on love for others.

LIST YOUR FAVORITE WAYS TO SHOW LOVE

We touch on how you like to receive love elsewhere in this book, but here our focus is on the reverse: how you like to give your love to others. We all have our own preferred methods of giving and receiving love, and that's okay! Noticing these preferences is a great way to appreciate your capacity for love and expand on the love you show the people in your life. Follow these steps to put together your list:

1. In your journal, turn to an empty page and write "How I Like to Show Love" at the top.
2. Now, think about some of your best and most cherished moments with those you love. Note how you showed them your love in each scenario. Perhaps you showed your love with gentle caresses, with words of affirmation and care, or with acts of service to others.
3. Look through these moments, label them with a descriptor of how you showed love, and browse to see what the patterns are; for example, you may generally show your dearest ones love through acts of thoughtfulness, but reserve physical touches for your significant other or your children.
4. Write down your top three to five ways to show love, and commit to putting these into practice more often. Refer to this list and show your loving ways whenever you feel you need a boost of love in your life.

PLAN OUT YOUR NEXT DISPLAY OF AFFECTION

It might sound odd, but planning out your next moves when it comes to showing your love for others can double the positive vibes: You get one boost of love and goodness when you plan it out, and another when you actually do it! As a bonus, the more time you spend thinking about and planning on giving love to those around you, the greater your capacity for experiencing love—for your family, your friends, and yourself. Try planning your next display of love and affection to boost your capacity for love.

1. First, pick a target for your love. Visualize them in your mind's eye, focusing on everything you love about them. Your spouse or significant other is a good pick for this, but it can be anyone you love.
2. Think about how you tend to show love. If you're not sure, check out the previous meditation (List Your Favorite Ways to Show Love). Also consider how your loved one likes to *receive* love.
3. Create a plan of (loving) attack. Decide on when you will strike (e.g., the next time you see them, at an upcoming event), what you will do to show them you love them, your timing, the location, and so on.
4. Run through the scenario in your head to make sure it works and to get the pre-attack rush of love and affection, then commit to going through with it!

VIEW LOVE AS AN INFINITE RESOURCE

How do you see love? Do you think of it as a finite resource—if you give too much love, you might run out? Some people see love that way, as something that you have only a limited amount to give, but the truth is that there is no limit on the love you can give away. In fact, the more love you give, the more you *have* to give! To change your perspective on love, give this meditation a try.

1. With your focus on yourself, think about how you see love. Really dig in and take a critical look at yourself; do you find yourself constantly sharing your love for people, or do you hold back for some reason?

2. Change your perspective and see love as something that is self-propagating. It's like one of those gadgets on office desks, where you pull one steel ball back and let it go, causing a chain reaction in a line of steel balls that creates infinite movement back and forth.

3. Imagine love as one of these gadgets. Pulling on one end and letting go is giving love, which causes the other end to jump and causes a wave of movement right back toward you, representing the love you receive. The more love you give, the more open you are to receiving love.

PRACTICE
"EYES WIDE OPEN" LOVE

You've certainly heard of the concept of unconditional love: a love that is not dependent on anything the recipient does. If you love someone unconditionally, it means you don't care what they've done or will do, you simply love them no matter what. While it's a popular topic for poets, unconditional love is not a common thing in our world—which might be a good thing. While unconditional love sounds great, it can manifest as an excuse to ignore bad behavior or unfairly idealize someone. Instead, try practicing "eyes wide open" love. This can be especially helpful for those in new relationships, but anyone can benefit from it.

1. Think about someone you love deeply. Visualize them in your mind, seeing all the wonderful things about them that make you love them so much.
2. Now, purposefully think about their flaws. Everyone has them! Think of at least three or four flaws or things that bother you.
3. With these flaws in mind, return to loving thoughts about them. Remind yourself that true love is love with "eyes wide open." It means that we see the person as they are, warts and all, and make a conscious decision to love them anyway. Also remind yourself that people can—and should—lose your love if they are toxic or abusive.
4. Practice "eyes wide open" love for all those you care deeply about, both to truly love them and to make healthy decisions about whom you love.

SEE LOVE
AS A VERB

We sometimes think of love as something that happens to us; we simply "fall in love" or "fall out of love"! It's often accompanied by a philosophy that we are bound to fate, and what happens to us is out of our hands. While the feeling of falling in love is fantastic, the truth is that we don't "fall in" true love, we *choose* to truly love someone. Adopting this perspective on love will make your relationships more stable and more satisfying, and contribute to a healthier and happier you. Try this meditation to get comfortable with this mindset.

1. Think about a time when you had a problem in your relationship. Maybe you did or said something that hurt your partner, or *didn't* do something that would have been good for your relationship.

2. Consider whether that was an unavoidable situation. Was there no other option available to you? Did you have no choice but to act as you did? You will almost certainly find that you did have a choice, but you made one that didn't turn out for the best.

3. Let this instance serve as an example of the truth: that love is a verb. To build deep, sustainable, long-lasting love, you need to consider your actions carefully and choose the ones that will contribute to your relationship rather than damage it.

4. Try to cement this new perspective in your mind, and commit to choosing to love in the future.

CUSTOMIZE HOW YOU SHOW LOVE

There's nothing wrong with showing your love for the important people in your life, but there are more effective and less effective ways to go about it. If you've ever heard of the Five Love Languages, you know that we all have our own preferences about how we give and receive love, and they will almost certainly not match up perfectly with our loved ones' preferences. Sometimes, we may show love to our cherished people, but it could be misinterpreted or not well received. Use this meditation as a guide in how to best show your affections to those you love.

1. Keep your awareness on yourself and think about how you like to receive love. What is most meaningful to you? What makes you feel most loved? Also think about when you received a show of love that was inappropriate or made you feel uncomfortable.

2. Now expand your awareness to others, and recognize that we all have our own favorite ways to receive love and times when we feel uncomfortable.

3. Pick a specific person and think about how they seem to like receiving love, and what they wouldn't like so much. Think of at least one way to successfully share your love with them and one way to avoid.

4. Now, promise to keep these preferences in mind when you interact with this person, and focus on another loved one the next time you try this meditation.

FORGIVE
SOMEONE YOU LOVE

Some say that forgiveness is the heart of love, and they're probably not far from the truth. Deep, lasting love is peppered with forgiveness on both sides. Although you might like to think your partner or friend would never hurt you, the truth is that the longer your relationships last, the more likely you are to hurt one another at some point—but one instance of pain does not doom a relationship. Use this meditation to work on building better relationships and being more giving with your love through forgiveness.

1. Think of someone you love who recently wronged you in some way. It shouldn't be a big transgression for the purposes of this meditation, but it should be something that you definitely felt hurt by.
2. Think of this person as a whole: You love them, so they probably have a ton of good qualities! Consider all the things you love about them and what makes them so loveable to begin with.
3. Now pair all their strengths with the hurt they caused you. Realize that this is the same person, and that their one transgression does not define them or how they feel about you.
4. Decide to forgive them, and extend your forgiveness out toward them right now.

RECOGNIZE THAT THE ROOT OF ALL LOVE IS THE SAME

You may be one of those people who find it easy-peasy to share your love with a spouse, a child, or a pet, but find it much more difficult to share your love with a friend or extended family member. If so, you're in luck—this meditation can help! Follow these steps to learn about the root of love and work on opening yourself up to give love more fully.

1. As you become centered and ready to meditate, turn your attention to the idea of love. Think about what love really is, what it looks like, how it feels in your heart.

2. Get down to the deepest depths of love and look at the roots. You'll find that love, no matter who the giver and who the receiver, all comes from the same place: an urge to connect with other people in a meaningful way. There are many different kinds of love, but they all have the same foundation.

3. That foundation is this: You care about the other person's well-being. This is at the basis of all types and shapes and sorts of love, whether it's romantic love, familial love, friendly love, or even love for strangers.

4. Remind yourself that since all love breaks down to this level, there is nothing that should hold you back from feeling and sharing love with those you care for most. Decide to be more open and giving with your love.

ACCEPT THE PAIN THAT COMES FROM LOVING SOMEONE

Usually, it feels wonderful to love someone and revel in that love. You feel warm and fuzzy inside, you feel as though you are made better through loving them, and you simply like to feel the intense, positive emotions that come with love. But if you want to work on being more giving and open to love, there's a reality that's good to accept: Loving someone means taking on their pain. Use this meditation to accept that fact and love fearlessly anyway.

1. Think about what happens when you love someone: You care about what they care about. You smile when they smile, you laugh when they laugh, but you also cry when they cry.
2. Remember that loving someone gives you incredible benefits, but that it also leaves you vulnerable to your loved one's pain. Think about a time when someone you loved was struggling, and remember how tough it was to see them struggle.
3. Now, remember what it was like when they rose above their struggle or overcame their challenges and you felt the high of success right along with them. Realize that the benefits of loving someone far outweigh the negatives.
4. Accept that to love means to laugh *and* cry with your loved one, and decide to love all the same.

CHAPTER 8

MEDITATIONS ON BEING RECEPTIVE

This chapter is focused on the idea of being receptive. This book has already touched on accepting love, but being receptive is a broader idea. It means being open to receiving things—from others, from yourself, from the universe at large. It can be easy to shut down your feeling side and walk through life with a closed mind and a closed heart, but this is not conducive to a healthy and happy you! You are at your best, your strongest, your most alive when you are able to open yourself up to everything this world has to give you. If you want to be able to accept love from others and from yourself and experience all that the universe has to offer, it pays to practice being receptive.

OPEN YOURSELF UP TO RECEIVING

It can be difficult for some of us to receive, whether we are being gifted with someone's time, a physical gift, a compliment, or even a random piece of good luck. When you are closed off from receiving, you have a very hard time appreciating and being compassionate toward yourself. These steps can help you open yourself up to receiving, whether it's receiving from the universe, a loved one, or your own generosity!

1. Grab your journal or a notebook and something to write with and take the steps to prepare yourself for meditation.
2. Think of at least three things you like about yourself. Write these down.
3. Think of at least three good things that have happened to you. Write these down as well.
4. Think of an opportunity you missed out on, preferably one that you could have easily taken advantage of if you were open to it.
5. Look over what you have written. Now, read the three things you like about yourself out loud, then end with, "I deserve to receive good things."
6. Read the three good things that happened to you out loud, then say, "I am able to receive good things."
7. Read the opportunity you missed out loud and finish with, "I will be open to receiving good things."

This simple exercise reminds you that you are worthy and capable of receiving good things and gives you permission to open yourself up to them in the future.

ALLOW OTHERS TO GIVE YOU FEEDBACK

A great way to open yourself up to receiving is to practice receiving feedback from others. It can be scary to get feedback on something, especially if it's something really personal to you, like a work of art, but closing yourself off from feedback is not a good option. It keeps you from being truly open and vulnerable, and it robs you of some great ideas and advice. To practice being more open to feedback, give this meditation a shot.

1. Think about what it means to get feedback from others. Does it make your efforts any less meaningful? Does it take away from the experience of creating whatever you produced? The answer is no, unless you allow that to happen.

2. Think about what goes through your mind when you provide feedback for others. Is your goal to hurt them, to tear them down, or to nitpick their work into oblivion? Of course not! Know that they have the same goals and sensitivities that you have when giving others feedback.

3. Decide to open yourself up to feedback. Pick one thing you'd like feedback on—something you're working on at your job, a side project, a piece of art you're producing—and pick one person to solicit comments from. Make sure it's someone who loves you and would be interested in giving feedback on this particular thing.

4. Promise yourself that you will accept their feedback without self-judgment and that you will not allow any feedback to hurt your self-esteem.

OPEN YOURSELF
TO THE UNIVERSE

Opening yourself up to others is a vital step on the way to being more receptive overall, but another important practice is to open yourself up to all the universe has to offer. After all, there are things you can receive from nature alone, like the calm that being in a beautiful setting provides or the awe that an intense thunderstorm can produce. Try this meditation to open yourself up to the universe.

1. Continue breathing deeply after your meditation prep. Take a few big breaths, hold them in for a second or two, then release them sharply and with intention.

2. Expand your awareness from yourself and your immediate surroundings. Go slowly, zooming out your internal camera. Pull back until you can see your whole house or the building you live in, then your neighborhood, then your town or city, then your state or country, etc., until you have zoomed out so far that the earth is no longer perceptible.

3. Think about all that this universe has to offer you. Think about the unsolved mysteries, the questions left unanswered—and the questions we haven't even thought to ask yet—and all the beautiful, wonderful things in the known universe.

4. Know that if you do not open yourself up to receiving from the universe, you will miss out on so many of these awesome experiences. Commit to staying open to receiving whatever the universe has in store for you.

TAKE IN YOUR SURROUNDINGS

Sometimes simply grounding yourself in the present moment can help you to be more receptive and open. That's what this meditation is all about: placing yourself in the context of this moment, here and now, and being open to what is around you. Follow these steps to help you take in your surroundings:

1. Open your eyes and look around you. Note where you are, what objects are near you, any people you can see, and the type of structure surrounding you (or the type of natural beauty, if you're outside).

2. Breathe deeply as you survey your surroundings, taking it all in. Look around as if you are seeing it for the first time, with the eyes of a newborn or perhaps a being not from this planet.

3. Think about what your surroundings can give you, starting with the easy stuff. The chair you're sitting in offers you a place to sit. The roof provides safety and security. But look closer, and you'll see more in-depth into what your surroundings provide: people to give you love, plants to supply you with oxygen, a painting to provide you with beauty or contemplation.

4. Open yourself up to your surroundings, and you'll find that there is much to receive. Give a quick thanks to the universe or the deity of your choice for these blessings.

TAKE A NATURE WALK
IN YOUR MIND

Nature walks are a wonderful way to boost your health—both physical and mental. Studies suggest that the more time we spend in nature, the better adjusted and happier we are; however, most of us can't leave our day job behind to spend all our days in nature! When you can't find the time for a walk in the woods, try taking a nature walk in your mind instead. You'll find that even imagining the experience makes you more open and receptive.

1. Keeping your eyes closed, imagine yourself on a path in the woods. See yourself walking along through the trees, looking around you and taking in all the natural beauty. Now put your perspective into the "you" in your mind's eye. See out of these eyes, and look around you.
2. As you move down this trail, take note of what you see. Observe the way the trees rustle and sway with the breeze, note the individual needles that make up the branch of a pine tree, and see the colorful flora that decorates the forest floor.
3. Engage your other senses: Notice the way the forest smells. Hear the sounds of birds chirping, branches rubbing, and squirrels chirruping back and forth.
4. Notice the sense of relaxation that your imagination can bring you, and thank yourself for being open to receiving it.

FOCUS ON
THE SOUNDS

If you're trying to get out of your own head and into being open to receiving, one of the simplest and easiest things to do is to engage your senses—in this case, engaging your hearing. When you get really invested in what you're doing—or the opposite, when you zone out completely—you tend to stop paying much attention to the signals you are receiving. To boost your mindfulness and become more open to life, practice this easy meditation.

1. Keep your eyes closed but redirect your attention to the information you're getting through your ears. Try to ignore anything you smell, taste, or feel, and focus all of your attention on sounds.

2. Try to tease apart the sounds you're hearing and label them. For example, instead of thinking "I hear traffic," think "I hear engines revving and idling" and "I hear car horns beeping" and "I hear tires screeching."

3. Consider how much you can learn about where you are and what is happening around you from sounds alone. Think about how wonderful it is to take in sounds. If the current ones aren't the most pleasant, think about pleasant sounds, like music and laughter.

4. Be grateful for your ability to hear, and decide to be more open and observant of all that you hear.

FOCUS ON
THE FEELS

If you're not up to date on today's slang, "feels" is shorthand for "feelings," but its connotations are a bit more complex. You might say you "caught the feels" if you start to like someone, or you might say that an inspiring and uplifting movie "gave you the feels." The truth is, "the feels" are all around us, but we sometimes close ourselves off from them. Instead of tuning them out, use this meditation to open yourself up to the feels.

1. Open your eyes while maintaining your slow, steady breathing. Look around you to find one thing that is personally meaning-ful or is attached to some sort of feeling for you. For example, if you're at home you might see a blanket that your spouse gave you or a framed picture of a loved one that has passed. If you're in a busy area, you might see a father walking hand in hand with his child.

2. Open yourself up to the feeling that this sight evokes in you, even if it's sadness. Remind yourself that it's okay to feel sad, disappointed, or any other emotion that's generally not en-couraged. Your feelings are valid, whatever they may be.

3. Close your eyes again and reflect on how accessible the feels are. Tell yourself that it's okay to feel, to be vulnerable, and set an intention to purposefully open yourself up to the feels every now and then.

MEDITATE ON NOURISHING YOUR BODY

Even if you're not the most open and receptive person, there is one way in which you are undoubtedly receptive: eating! Just like being open to sights, sounds, feelings, and ideas, we frequently open ourselves up to experience our food. To expand on your receptiveness to what you eat, think about what is actually happening when you take in food.

1. First, think about the journey your food takes when you eat. You open your mouth and choose to ingest food, chew it, and swallow it, then it travels down your throat, through your esophagus, and all the way into your stomach and intestines. Here, it's broken down and absorbed by your body, which then turns it into the energy you need to keep your body running.

2. Allow yourself to feel some awe at the amazing way your body works. Remember that this happens to each bite you take of any food you eat.

3. Think about what you are doing when you open yourself up to food: nourishing your body and giving it everything it needs to get you where you need to go and do what you need to do.

4. Expand on this idea, and consider that everything you take in has the potential to nourish you in some way. Words can nourish your soul, ideas can nourish your mind, and physical touches can nourish your heart. Just as you are open to food, stay open to everything else you can receive!

MEDITATE TO ACCEPT CRITICISM—CAREFULLY

If you're looking to get better at accepting feedback in general, try the exercise Allow Others to Give You Feedback earlier in this chapter. If you're working on being better at accepting criticism specifically, you're in the right place! It's not always easy to accept criticism from others, but it's vital that you build the capacity to do so. Whether you want to or not, you will inevitably be the target of criticism at some point. Use this meditation to practice being receptive to it without being *too* affected by it.

1. Consider what it means to truly consider criticism directed at you. Does it necessarily mean that you agree with the criticism? Or that you are somehow "less" because of it? Does it automatically invalidate the things in your "pro" column? Of course this is not an inevitable product of being open to criticism.
2. Remind yourself of what it *does* mean to be open to criticism: You admit that you don't always do the right thing in exactly the right way, that you are not all-knowing, and that you have room for self-improvement.
3. Accept that criticism is not always a bad thing, and make the decision to be open to it—at least when it is delivered without malice or ulterior motive!

STORE UP GOOD VIBES

Good vibes are the positive emotions, the sense of success, and the warm, fuzzy feelings you get from pleasant experiences throughout your day. Even if you feel like you don't run into good vibes often, you probably encounter them more than you realize. To help you stay open to good vibes, follow this guide.

1. Think back through your day, filtering for the good moments. If you're meditating in the morning, think about the previous day. What good things happened? What moments did you enjoy? Did anything particularly fun or exciting happen to you?
2. For each moment you think of, no matter how big or small, imagine the good vibes that it created. It may have given you a quick mood boost, made you smile, or just perked you up momentarily.
3. Think about how many good vibes you experienced. See all of them in your mind's eye. Now, consider this: Those good vibes don't pop up then immediately fade away—they stick around for a while! If you want, you can choose to keep them around for days, weeks, even months or years. Imagine how many good vibes you'd have if you decided to keep them all!
4. Commit to being open and receptive to good vibes for the rest of the day. Look for them, seek them out, and store them in a little bucket or box in your mind for you to pull from later.

BE MINDFUL OF
THE LITTLE THINGS

They say "Don't sweat the small stuff," and that's great advice—it's good not to get down about the little things! However, the less oft-repeated phrase, "It's the little things that count," can be equally as important. Joy is not found in momentous occasions alone; real, lasting joy is found in noticing and appreciating the little things. To practice keeping yourself open to the little things, try some mindfulness meditation.

1. Begin by bringing your awareness to yourself. Note how you're feeling and whether anything is on your mind. If there is something big on your mind, consciously choose to put it in a box for later. Right now you need your full concentration on the little stuff, not the big stuff.

2. Next, turn your focus to little things that make you happy. What brings a smile to your face or gives you pep in your step? For example, this author finds immense joy in seeing a cute dog, watching the little displays of affection between couples, and seeing someone donate or give a kind word to a person who is homeless or struggling.

3. Make an internal list of all the little things that build you up and cheer you up. Go through the list and promise yourself to be more mindful of each of these little things.

OPEN
YOUR HEART

If you struggle with being open and receptive, visualization can help you move past mental blocks and break down barriers without tackling them head on—it's like rerouting yourself to avoid those silly obstacles to begin with. This visualization can be a powerful one for anyone who feels shut off or closed down for whatever reason, as it works on opening you up at the core. Follow these steps to try it for yourself:

1. Keeping your eyes firmly shut, visualize your heart. Don't worry if you don't know exactly what a heart looks like—the important thing is that you have a good image in your head that represents your heart, not that it's an anatomically correct image!

2. See your heart as a closed system, not accepting anything into it. Think about everything you miss out on by keeping it closed up tight.

3. Visualize slowly and carefully opening your heart up. See it unfold like a flower in your chest, becoming open to all the good things around you. Imagine the love of your friends and family, happiness and joy, inspiration and awe, all flowing into your heart.

4. Know that opening your heart up like this is a mental and emotional exercise you can do to keep your heart open and healthy. Commit to practicing this technique at least once a week.

COMMIT TO
LISTENING ATTENTIVELY

When you listen to others speak, how well would you say you listen? Do you ever find yourself zoning out, or perhaps formulating your response in your head before they even finish making their point? Don't feel bad; we all do this sometimes! But the difference between a mediocre conversationalist and a great person to talk to really comes down to your skill at listening. The more open you are to taking in information from others, the more you will understand and the better able you will be to connect with them. Try this meditation to commit to listening attentively and becoming a better conversationalist, friend, and family member.

1. Think about what it means to listen attentively. It involves not just listening, but listening carefully: hearing the words the other person is saying and looking for the intent behind them. It means you are not simply waiting for your turn to speak, but attempting to take in all that your conversation partner is offering you.
2. Consider how good it feels when someone listens attentively to you. You probably find yourself drawn to speaking with this person, because he or she makes you feel heard.
3. Make a conscious decision to become an attentive listener and share that good feeling with others. Set an intention to listen carefully, fully, and attentively to what others have to say.

MEDITATE ON
A NEW IDEA

One of the most effective ways to keep yourself open to receiving is to purposefully expose yourself to new ideas. When you are frequently getting new insights and learning useful lessons from the ideas you encounter, it's easier to stay open and receptive to all that life has to offer you. Try this meditation to keep being receptive to new things.

1. Think of a new idea you recently heard. It could be a new idea at work, the basis of a new study you read about, or just a "shower thought" from a friend. Get a good handle on exactly what the thought is.

2. Now flesh it out. Follow the idea down the rabbit hole. Think thoughts that start with "What if..." and "If that's true, then..." and "That suggests..." Give the idea your sole attention for a few minutes.

3. Come back to being present and in the moment, then do a quick self-assessment. Do you feel any more creative? Do you feel that you might have tapped into more expansive thinking? Are you considering possibilities and feeling open and non-judgmental about your thoughts? Hopefully you are!

4. Embrace the feeling of being receptive and curious, and remind yourself to stay open to new ideas when you hear them.

OPEN YOURSELF
TO SELF-COMPASSION

For the final entry in this chapter, we'll focus on moving directly toward our goal: being more open to self-compassion. If you have tried the other meditations in this chapter and had success, you should be ready to go straight to the heart of the matter: being receptive to compassion for yourself. Follow these instructions to practice opening yourself to self-compassion.

1. Think of a recent challenge or disappointment you faced that really threw you for a loop. Think about how it affected you, and what you faced in overcoming it. Remember how it felt to struggle.

2. Place your hands over your heart center (on your chest, slightly to the left of the midline of your body), and use a little bit of pressure to give you the sensation of being gently held.

3. Allow yourself to empathize with your struggling past self. Say, "I'm sorry, self. I know that was hard for you."

4. Next, invest in your self-compassion and expand on it. Repeat these sentiments to yourself:

   * May I be free from harm.
   * May I overcome my obstacles.
   * May I feel peace.
   * May I experience joy.
   * May I be healthy and happy.

5. Close with a deep, cleansing breath and a promise to be more compassionate toward yourself.

CHAPTER 9

MEDITATIONS ON BEING PRESENT

If you're a practitioner of mindfulness, you know the benefits of staying present. If you're new to mindfulness, don't worry! The first meditation in this chapter is a good place to start. Being mindful is a great way to stay aware of your thoughts and feelings and keep in touch with yourself, which opens the door to more acceptance, love, and compassion for yourself. These meditations are heavy on the mindfulness but include other techniques too, like visualization, noting your most problematic distractions, focusing on the positive, self-reflection, replacing triggers with reminders to be mindful and compassionate, and even dealing with your cravings in a positive way. Any of these meditations will help you stay in the present and focused on enjoying your own company.

PRACTICE
BASIC MINDFULNESS

There are a million ways you can use mindfulness to stay present and engaged in the moment, but it's a good idea to start with the basics. This meditation will walk you through mindfulness meditation and teach you how to start becoming present more often. Once you've got the hang of it, you can expand, add to, alter, and adjust the experience however you'd like! Follow these steps to start your practice:

1. Start your meditation practice as you normally do, in a comfortable seated position and with limited distractions. Turn your focus to your breath and breathe steadily and with intention.

2. Now, take the awareness from your breath to yourself. Take note of how you feel in this moment, both your body and your mind. Observe your thoughts and feelings like an unbiased scientist observing a specimen. Notice your thoughts as they enter your mind and let them slide out just as easily.

3. Next, turn your attention to your surroundings. Take note of what you see, what you hear, what you smell, and what you taste. Be cognizant of what is happening around you, and place yourself firmly within your present context.

4. Engage in the moment, and let yourself simply be in the here and now.

That's it! Now you have practiced basic mindfulness.

NOTICE
YOUR ENVIRONMENT

To take your mindfulness practice further and become even more present in your current surroundings, you can focus your session on your environment. When you connect with your current environment, you allow yourself to actively live your life and enjoy the moment. The more you can stay out of your head and in the moment, the easier it will be to cultivate positive associations with simply being with yourself.

1. Start out with a basic mindfulness meditation, but expand on the environment piece. Don't just take a quick peek at your surroundings; instead, make a long, slow sweep, dedicating yourself to not missing a thing.

2. Look all around you, even behind you (as a bonus, you can get in a good stretch while you do this). Notice everything there is to see, down to the chips in the paint on the wall, the texture of the rug, and the thin layer of dust on your ceiling fan.

3. See everything around you, but make sure to keep an open and nonjudgmental attitude. Don't evaluate or rate or criticize what you see; simply note it and move on. That layer of dust is not an indication of your cleanliness; it's simply something that exists in your current environment.

4. Allow your thoughts as you look around you to rise to your consciousness, then let them fade away as new thoughts replace them. Don't hold on to any of your thoughts, simply focus on being where you are right now.

FIND THREE
PLEASANT THINGS

This is a slightly different way to practice being present, as it emphasizes being present and *positive* at the same time. It's a great way to focus yourself if you find yourself zoning out as you notice your surroundings. It will help you stay open and positive instead of making a mindless sweep of the room. Use this meditation to try your hand at being present and positive.

1. When you're ready to begin, open your eyes and look around you. For this meditation, don't worry about being impartial or nonjudgmental; instead, be on the lookout for things that you judge to be pleasant.
2. Pick the first pleasant thing you see. You might be drawn to a flower, your pet snoozing on the floor, or a memento from a fun trip on your desk. Focus on the pleasant thing for a minute, soaking it all in. Cultivate gratitude for this pleasant thing in your life, and be happy that you are here right now to enjoy it.
3. Repeat this process for two more pleasant things.
4. At the end, list your three pleasant things and send up some gratitude for having three good things to notice around you. Thank yourself for being present enough to notice them.

FOCUS YOUR ATTENTION ON A FRIEND

If you've been regularly practicing mindfulness and staying present, this can be a good next step: staying present even with the distraction of a friend. Friends can help us stay present in the moment, but occasionally even the most beloved of friends gets only half of our attention, while the rest is running through scenarios in our head or planning our next meal. To stay in the moment, practice focusing on your friend.

1. You probably won't get to prepare for this meditation as you normally do, but that's okay. It's a new challenge! Keep your eyes and ears open but let yourself sink into the present moment. Notice what is happening around you and ground yourself firmly in the present.

2. Now, turn that attention toward your friend. Listen with intention to what your friend is saying, but expand your awareness to include the bigger picture.

3. Take note of what your friend is wearing today. Notice if they did their hair or makeup differently, if they got new glasses, or if they're wearing a new watch.

4. Think about the good qualities your friend is displaying right now. Are they talking passionately about one of their favorite topics? Are they entertaining you with a story or delighting you with a joke? Notice what you love about your friend in this moment.

5. Continue to engage with your friend, but hold on to one fragment or thought that came up, and share it with them later in the conversation (e.g., "Hey, I love your new watch!").

SAVOR
A SNACK

If you're a foodie, you'll love this meditation! It employs a fun technique: savoring a tasty treat to stay present and in the moment. Think about how effective this can be. I'm willing to bet you have had at least a few moments where you interrupted someone or felt like you were jolted to attention after taking a bite of something unexpectedly good. A positive food experience is an unparalleled joy in life! Use this to your advantage and let it help you stay present.

1. Before you begin preparing for your meditation, pick out a sweet treat or a salty, savory snack. It can be anything, but the meditation works best if it's something you're excited to eat.

2. Go through your normal pre-meditation process, then open your eyes and prepare to snack!

3. Hold your snack, thinking about how it feels. Is it soft and creamy? Crispy? Squishy?

4. Bring it up to your nose and take a deep breath, inhaling the scent. Savor the scent, letting it bring up any associated memories that want to pop up—after all, smell is the sense most closely tied to memories!

5. Finally, take a small bite. Bite slowly and chew thoughtfully. Notice the texture, how it feels in your mouth, and how it changes as you chew. Notice the individual flavors that make up the overall taste, and savor each and every one of them. Stay present and, most importantly, enjoy your snack!

BREATHE MINDFULLY

Although the meditation prep at the beginning of this book provides a handy guide for focusing on your breathing, it's only referenced as a small part of getting into the right headspace for meditating. To practice more extended control of your breath, this meditation is a great tool. Give it a try by following these steps:

1. Once you're ready, continue to focus on your breathing. Really feel each inhale: the air entering through your nostrils, traveling down your throat, through the trachea, and into your lungs, filling every corner. Then focus on each exhale: pushing the air out of your lungs as they squeeze together, forcing the air up your throat and out through your nostrils again.

2. As you breathe, try to leave any self-consciousness behind. Allow your inhales and exhales to make noise. Take up space as you breathe. Don't think about the way your belly expands when you inhale or whether you have a double chin when you exhale.

3. Continue breathing steadily, but begin to play with your breath. Take long, slow breaths, and sharp, quick exhales. Try pausing for a second or two between each inhale and exhale. Pay attention to how your breathing affects your energy level and your mood.

4. End with another set of deep, cleansing breaths.

This meditation keeps you present and in the moment, and helps you leave your self-focused anxieties behind.

TAKE A
MEDITATIVE STROLL

If you have a nice place to take a walk nearby, consider trying an active meditation. Although most meditation happens in a seated position, there's nothing stopping you from meditating as you walk. The benefit of practicing meditation on the go is that you can easily stay present in multiple scenarios, not just while you are quietly seated in a distraction-free environment. This presence will help you stay connected with yourself, making it easy to offer yourself love and compassion in the moment.

1. You can prepare for your meditation as usual or do it all during your walk, whichever you'd prefer. If you prepare as you walk, go through all the same steps but while your eyes are open and your feet are moving.

2. When you're feeling centered, shift your gaze to the horizon. See what is in front of you, and think about what you're walking toward. Walk toward it with purpose.

3. Next, turn your attention to your feet. Pay attention to your gait, and feel every sensation as your feet rise and fall with each step. Think about how it feels in your body as you walk. Notice which muscles you use and how it feels to use them.

4. Focus on your movement for a few minutes and be present in your walk, then end with a quick thanks for legs to carry you and the ability to walk. Then give yourself some gratitude for doing something good for you.

CHOOSE AN OBJECT
TO CONCENTRATE ON

If you find it tough to stay present when there's so much to see, hear, touch, and do—when distractions abound and you can't tune them out—this meditation can show you another technique to stay present. Instead of trying to be aware of everything, be very aware of one thing. Once you practice this enough, it will be easier to expand that awareness to more objects, to yourself, and to your general environment.

1. As you settle in for your meditation session, open your eyes and look around you. Find one object that you like to look at, or that holds your interest for some reason. It might be the most brightly colored or oddly shaped object, or it might hold personal meaning to you. Whatever you choose, fix your gaze on it.

2. Focus your awareness on noticing everything there is to notice about this object. See its shape, its curves or edges. Notice its color, taking note of whether it's solid or has many colors. Look for any observable patterns, swirls, or gradients. See its texture if you can, and think about how it feels to touch it.

3. Spend a minute or two focusing on the object, drinking it all in. Stay aware of yourself and your presence as you do.

4. Finally, expand your awareness to notice the object in its context. See what's around it and what's around you, using the experience to bring yourself fully into the present.

HEIGHTEN YOUR
BODY AWARENESS

How much time do you spend just *being* in your body? You probably take note of what's happening in your body when you're in pain
or when you're at the gym. Is it only times like these that you're fully
aware? Most of us so rarely just simply experience and appreciate being in our own body. Use this meditation to boost your body presence.

1. As you finish your meditation prep, turn your attention back to
   your body. Send all of your awareness into it, reaching out to
   each corner and nook and cranny.
2. Scan your body for any aches, pains, or sore spots. Make note
   of each pain point, then continue your scan.
3. Next, notice anywhere in your body that feels particularly
   good. If you just worked out and have that deliciously tired
   feeling or just walked out of a massage appointment, you'll
   likely have some spots that feel really good right now! Notice
   where you feel strong, relaxed, or comfortably stretched.
4. Now, focus on the sensations that are more difficult to notice,
   like the feeling of your legs pressing into your chair or your hands
   resting lightly on your knees. Notice all the sensations you can
   find and meet them with a curious but not judgmental attitude.
5. Congratulate yourself for being present and mindful in your
   own body, and commit to doing it more often.

EMBRACE NOT KNOWING ALL THE ANSWERS

Sure, you know some things, but there's a whole lot you don't know and probably never will. As much as we may like to learn about new things, there will always be topics about which we are completely oblivious. In addition, there are some things that are simply unknowable. If you're like me, this can sometimes drive you crazy and get you stuck in your own head instead of living in the moment. To combat this, try this meditation on embracing the state of "not knowing."

1. After your meditation prep, take one more deep breath, breathing slowly in and slowly out. Get as settled as you can and turn your attention to what you know.

2. Think about all that you know, the knowledge that it has taken you an entire lifetime to gain. You know a lot!

3. Now think about how much there is to know: There are more than seven billion people on the planet, each with their own set of knowledge gained over a lifetime. Next, imagine what *none of us* know! There are things that nobody knows for sure, and certainly things we don't even know that we don't know.

4. Think about what a teeny, tiny drop in the bucket your own knowledge is compared to this vast amount of knowledge. Accept that this is your natural state, and worrying about it isn't going to change a thing. Commit to staying out of your head and in the moment.

IDENTIFY YOUR
TOP DISTRACTIONS

We all get distracted sometimes, and there's no cure for many of our distractions—life is simply full of them! However, there may be some things that you find are constant or repeat distractions, but they're not inevitable. Identifying your distraction triggers is the first step toward taking action to negate or mitigate them, which is what this meditation is focused on. Follow these steps to give it a try:

1. At the end of your day, prepare for meditation as you usually do, but make sure to grab a journal or notebook to jot down some notes in.

2. Once you're settled in, look back over your day (or the last week, if that helps). Think about each time you were starting to get in the flow of your current activity but something distracted you. What interrupted you? Write it down.

3. Now, consider your list. Think about how often each of these things happens during a typical day. Do some of them happen more often than others? If so, order them according to frequency: most frequent at the top of the list, least frequent at the bottom.

4. Take a look at your top distraction triggers and consider whether there's any way to work around them. For example, if your top trigger is the notification sound from your phone, consider putting it on silent periodically.

5. Now, put your strategy into practice and enjoy staying more present!

REFLECT ON YOUR DAY

Reflection is a great technique to add to your regular practice. No matter what your goal is, a little self-reflection can help! It might seem paradoxical to reflect on your day in order to be more mindful, but it's about boosting your overall mindfulness: Reflecting on your day will take you out of the present, but just for a moment, and reflecting will help you determine how present you really are and how well you're doing in meeting your goal. Use the following guide to try this meditation.

1. Think back over your day. Try to "rewind" in your head, all the way back to the morning, and watch the video playing at a quick pace in your head.
2. First, look through the video for evidence of being present. When did you find yourself totally present and observant of what was happening around you? When did you notice something interesting in your surroundings? Did you ever have a moment when you identified a feeling or emotion that you normally wouldn't?
3. Give yourself a pat on the back for these moments! Congratulate yourself on the moments when you were mindful.
4. Now look back over your day, but with an eye out for moments when you could have been present and were *not* present. Think of some ways that you could have encouraged yourself to practice mindfulness in these moments and keep them in mind to try tomorrow.

CHOOSE A CHORE
AND DO IT MINDFULLY

Pick a chore, any chore! It doesn't matter what activity you choose for this meditation, but it should be something you do regularly (e.g., washing the dishes, vacuuming, mowing the lawn). If it's something you don't particularly *love* doing, that can give the meditation an added benefit. Follow these steps to practice doing your chore mindfully:

1. As you prepare to meditate, get ready to do your chore as well. For example, you might start running the water to get it hot or digging the vacuum cleaner out of the closet as you prepare.

2. Once you're ready, get started on your activity of choice; however, instead of doing it mindlessly or getting it over with as quickly as possible, think about each step as you're doing it. For example, as you run the sponge over the plate in your hand, think about what you're trying to accomplish right now and how well you're doing it.

3. As you continue through your chore, keep focusing on what you're doing and doing it well, but also think about how it feels while you're doing it. Do you notice any specific sensations, like the slimy feel of grease on that plate or the pull in your biceps from vacuuming?

4. Stay present and keep focused on doing your chore well, and you will not only do it better—you might even start to enjoy it!

REPLACE
A TRIGGER

What are your triggers? Is there anything that simply *always* makes you mad or sad? Or perhaps there's something that instantly brings up some mild—but persistent—irritation (i.e., a pet peeve). It's too bad that we have so many triggers to negative and unpleasant states of mind. Wouldn't it be great to have something that sets us off toward a more positive state of mind instead of a negative one? Well, good news: You can create a positive trigger like this for yourself! All you need is a little bit of practice, and you can turn a negative trigger into a positive one.

Here's how:

1. Think about what triggers you and puts you into a negative mood or state of mind. It could be just about anything, but we'll use the example of being cut off in traffic.
2. Imagine you were just cut off in traffic. How do you feel? Angry, upset, outraged? Or maybe just a little annoyed?
3. Instead of resigning yourself to getting upset every time you get cut off in traffic, choose to use it as a reminder to be present. It's a great reminder to be present, especially since the person who cut you off is probably *not* acting very mindfully, and you can see the consequences of that reality.
4. Commit to using each instance of getting cut off to pause (your emotions, not your car!), be grateful that no one was hurt, and focus on being in the present moment.

TAKE ADVANTAGE
OF YOUR CRAVINGS

If you have any cravings from quitting smoking, swearing off alcohol, or any other craving-inducing substance or activity, you actually have a fantastic built-in reminder to be present and compassionate to yourself throughout the day. You might not feel lucky to be quitting something that's so hard to give up, but at least you can take advantage of this little silver lining. Read on to learn how.

1. When you're feeling centered and relaxed, turn your thoughts toward what it feels like to experience a craving. Think about the thoughts that pop up, the emotions that arise, and how it feels in your body. For example, if you're craving a cigarette, you might think, "Just this once," feel a little desperate or stressed, and even feel a little shaky or light-headed.

2. Remind yourself that in these moments, you cannot control how you feel—but you can control how you respond to your feelings. The craving might make it feel impossible to resist, but all it can do is influence your mood; ultimately, you are in control of your behavior.

3. Instead of giving in to the craving, use it as a reminder to practice mindfulness and extend yourself some love. It's hard to quit anything, and it will naturally make you moody, irritable, and generally just feeling down in the dumps. Along with being present, give yourself a little love and respect for doing such a difficult thing.

CHAPTER 10

MEDITATIONS FOR SELF-CARE

Self-care and meditation go hand in hand; self-care can involve meditation, and meditation can also be focused on self-care. Combining the two just makes sense, and doing both at once can give you a leg up on building and maintaining the self-compassion you want to cultivate. When you take good care of yourself, it's easier to see yourself as worthy of compassion and deserving of love. In this chapter, you will find several ways to take care of yourself and show yourself love, including meditating on gratitude, identifying your needs, reliving relaxing experiences, taking a mindful walk, trying a nice, warm shower meditation, and using visualization to boost your self-acceptance and self-love.

RELIVE A
BUBBLE BATH

One of the great things about meditation is that meditating on an experience can bring you some of the same benefits as actually engaging in that experience. Visualization is a powerful tool that can essentially trick your mind into thinking it experienced whatever you visualized. To take advantage of this benefit, try reliving a relaxing bubble bath in your meditation. It will help you improve your visualization skills and give you some self-care at the same time.

1. Think back to your most recent bubble bath. If you don't take many bubble baths or can't even think of a single bubble bath you've taken, put your imagination to work!
2. Construct the scene in detail. Think about where you were (i.e., which bathroom or bathtub), when you took the bath, what candles you had burning or scents were in the air, and what bubbles you used. Bring forth as much detail as you can.
3. Slip into the scenario you built. Feel the warm water as you step into the tub. Remember how it felt as you slid into the tub and the water covered your body. Feel it instantly erasing your aches and soothing your pains. Play with the bubbles and feel the slippery, soapy sensation on your hands.
4. Sit back and relax for a few minutes. Let the peace wash over you and let out a sigh of relief.

PLAN OUT YOUR
NEXT THERAPY SESSION

If you're a proponent of self-care, you may also be a frequent visitor to your therapist's office. Therapy is an integral part of self-care for many people, and lots of clients learn about self-care through their therapist, making the two closely linked. To get a boost of self-care and plan for even *more* self-care in your future, try this meditation involving planning out your next therapy session. Here's how it works:

1. As you enter your relaxed and centered state, turn your awareness to yourself. Think about how important it is to take good care of yourself, and remind yourself of when your next therapy appointment is.
2. Now, think about what you'll discuss at your appointment. Are there things that have been bothering you lately? Are there certain issues from your past that have been cropping up? Or perhaps you just want to work on some new skills.
3. Think about what is most important for you right now and what will help you meet your challenges or achieve your long-term goals. Come up with a couple of short-term goals for your next appointment based on these needs.
4. Consider how vital your therapy sessions are to your mental health and congratulate yourself for going, then commit to bringing up your planned discussion topics the next time you see your therapist.

VISUALIZE GIVING
YOURSELF A HUG

Visualization is an effective tool for changing your attitude about yourself. It can be even more impactful when you place a copy of yourself in the visualization. It's the only way we get to interface with ourselves on a face-to-face basis (although the mirror gives us a little taste of it), which can be a powerful technique. Walk yourself through this guided visualization to give the technique a try.

1. Start by visualizing yourself. You don't need anything fancy, just see yourself as you are, standing in a safe and comfortable space.
2. Now, insert a copy of yourself. This copy not only looks like you, it is an exact replica, down to the molecules. You should now see two of the exact same person—you—in your mind's eye.
3. Watch your copy walk up to your original version and listen as they ask for a hug, then hear your original self agree. Watch as your copy reaches out toward and embraces your original self.
4. As you visualize the hug, allow yourself to feel it. Feel the familiar, loving arms wrap around you. Listen to your copy as they tell you they love you, that you are okay exactly as you are, and that you deserve to be happy and well.
5. Keep the embrace going as long as you'd like, but make sure to visualize the end: Your two selves pull apart and smile at one another with nothing but love in their eyes.

TRY OUT
A MANTRA

If you've never used a mantra before, this is a great time to give it a try! Mantras are short phrases or words that you can repeat to keep yourself grounded and focused on your goals. Your mantra can be anything you'd like, but it should be positive, easy to remember, and sure to prompt you into the desired behavior or thought pattern. Use this meditation to create a mantra for yourself and test it out.

1. As you reach your meditation headspace, expand your awareness a bit to think about what your current goal is; it is likely along the lines of self-compassion (or else you'd be reading another book!), so it might be something simple like, "Learn to love myself more" or "Cultivate greater compassion toward myself when I make a mistake."

2. Based on your goal, think of a short phrase or word that aligns with your goal. For example, if your goal is to learn to love yourself more, your mantra might be "self-love."

3. Try out your proposed mantra to see if it works. Quietly repeat the mantra a few times to yourself, seeing how it feels. If it feels right, continue to chant it as you focus your attention back on your breath. Let the words seep into you, filling you up and leaving no room for self-doubt or anxiety.

Remember your mantra and use it when you need a reminder or when you just want to get closer to your goal.

MEDITATE ON GRATITUDE

Gratitude is a wonderful thing to feel and an even more wonderful thing to practice. Gratitude that is intentional, purposeful, and practiced regularly is life-changing for many people, changing their perspective from "what's wrong here" to "what's right here." To focus on "what's right here" and increase your capacity for self-love and self-compassion, give this meditation a try.

1. Slowly expand your awareness to yourself and your life. Put on a positive lens and comb through your life to find that which is good, fulfilling, engaging, and life-giving.
2. Note at least five to ten things that are good in your life, things that make you feel lucky to be alive.
3. Practice gratitude for these things, and give thanks that you get to experience such wonderful things in your life.
4. From here, expand your boundaries to think about the grander things: your heartbeat, your lungs to fill with breath, your legs to carry you where you want to go, your brain for its capacity to meditate in the first place, etc.
5. Stretch your gratitude as far as it will go and feel thankful for the gift of life. Be grateful for the opportunity to live this life and experience all it has to offer. Dedicate yourself to be more focused on gratitude from now on, even if it's just a minute or two a day.

IDENTIFY
YOUR NEEDS

Self-care is vital to a self-loving, self-compassionate you, but you may not know the specifics to *your* self-care. There are a lot of general suggestions on ways to care for yourself, but one person's self-care ritual may be an arduous or downright boring task to another. To reach a healthy level of self-care, you need to figure out what works for you, and that's what this meditation will help you do.

1. Keep your eyes closed and continue to focus on yourself. Think about times when you have felt calmest and happiest.
2. Now, think about what contributed to you feeling calm and happy. Was it doing a crossword puzzle? Having a beer after dinner? Hitting the gym?
3. Write down anything that comes to mind. You should be able to write down at least five to ten activities that help you re-center.
4. Now, take a look at your list and see if you can identify some common themes. Are most of your items related to relaxing (e.g., bubble bath, nap, an hour of guilty-pleasure TV)? Or do you see a trend of physical activity (e.g., lifting weights, going for a run, yoga)?
5. Note the trend(s) and boil them down to find your needs. For example, you might have a need for relaxation or a need to move your body.
6. Now that you know your needs, you're ready to figure out how to meet them!

COUNT TO TEN— AND COUNT AGAIN

It's a simple but time-honored technique: counting to ten. You can use it to defuse your anger, pause and think before reacting, and get centered when you feel a strong emotion; however, you can also use it to manage your emotions and bring yourself to a place of self-love and self-compassion. Follow these steps to try this easy but effective technique.

1. With your eyes closed and your mind centered, call to mind a moment of self-doubt you had recently. It should be a moment when you really struggled to accept and love yourself how you'd like to.

2. If you can, try to bring up the same feelings you felt in the moment. Put yourself in your earlier self's shoes and remember what it felt like to deal with that self-doubt.

3. Now, instead of giving in to the self-doubt, press the pause button in your mind. Clear your head as best you can and count to ten. If it helps, you can use one of the devices to count in roughly equal one-second intervals (e.g., "one-Mississippi, two-Mississippi").

4. Once you reach ten, re-evaluate. Are you still feeling dragged down by self-doubt, or did it lift a bit? If you're still clutched in the grips of self-doubt, repeat the count and re-evaluate at the end.

5. Continue counting to ten until you're in a better place and able to use another tactic to produce more loving and caring feelings toward yourself.

TAKE A RESTORATIVE
NATURE WALK

Nature is a powerful cure for a lot of what ails us. Our ancestors spent all of their time in nature; it's only recently that humans started living mostly indoors. Given the tiny fraction of time that humans have spent living inside, it's no wonder that we miss being in nature when we've been cooped up in our homes or in the city for too long! To rectify this issue, try taking a mindful, nature-focused walk. It's best to find a place where you can be truly immersed in nature, but any place with some trees or other plants will do in a pinch!

1. Prep for your meditation session as usual, then open your eyes but try to keep yourself in the same frame of mind. Set off toward your destination while staying calm, centered, and mindful.

2. As you walk, look around you. Take it all in—everything you see, everything you hear, and everything you notice with your other senses. Touch a fern or a tree trunk as you walk by it, smell the sap or the flowers you pass by, and keep your ears perked for birdsong or rushing water.

3. Let the natural calm and sense of order in the scenery infuse you. Immerse yourself in it and let it settle into your heart as a valued guest. Continue the walk for as long as you'd like, but try to stay mindful the whole time.

TRY A SHOWER MEDITATION

If you haven't meditated in the shower yet, you're missing out! It's an excellent opportunity to unwind, relax, and refresh. Sometimes all you need to feel better is a few minutes under warm water to feel clean and happy, but adding a meditation component pairs the physical comfort of a shower with the soul-rejuvenating power of meditating.

1. Turn the shower on to your desired temperature and prepare to meditate as you get ready for the shower. As you undress, focus on your breathing and how your body feels. As you step in, expand your awareness to your immediate surroundings and give yourself over to the experience.

2. Stand underneath the showerhead, allowing the water to run over your head and your face. Feel it wash away the grime of the day. As the water flows down your body, feel any impurities being swept away with it.

3. Turn so the stream is focused on your back, and let it give you a mini water massage. Stand still for a few minutes, not cleaning yourself or rushing to get through it, but simply enjoying the sensations. Notice how it feels as the water hits your shoulders and cascades down your back.

4. Cultivate a sense of gratitude for this simple but oh-so-lovely pleasure of a hot shower. Embrace feeling clean and fresh and new, step out, and go on with your day—but carry that calm, meditative state with you when you go.

GIVE YOURSELF
A MINI MASSAGE

Giving yourself a massage is generally a much less relaxing activity than getting a massage from a professional, but it can still be a relaxing and enjoyable experience. Plus, massaging yourself allows for another benefit: boosting your self-love. We tend to only give physical affection to those we are very close and intimate with, which means we generally associate such caresses with love. When you show yourself this type of love, it can act as a good reminder that you love and care for yourself just as you do for others.

1. As you finish your meditation preparations, keep your eyes shut and your focus on your body. Note any areas where you have pain or soreness.
2. Start with a simple caress: Place your hands on your upper arms (left hand on right arm, right arm on left arm) and rub slowly up and down your arms. Give a little squeeze at the shoulders if that feels good.
3. Reach up a little farther and give yourself a shoulder massage. Spend another minute here, then move on to your neck.
4. Next, move down to your thighs. Give them each a gentle rubdown, then move farther down to your calves and shins.
5. End with your feet, giving each a solid minute or two of attention. Give your feet some extra love for supporting you throughout your day.
6. Thank yourself for the loving touch, open your eyes, and continue with your day.

CREATE
A RITUAL

The word "ritual" might make you think of things more formal than self-care, but a ritual isn't constrained to things like religious ceremonies or summoning spirits; it can also be something that you decide is important to you and that you would like to do mindfully and purposefully, with the express purpose of benefiting you. For example, you might turn your morning coffee into a ritual. Now, instead of simply getting your daily dose of caffeine each morning, you will engage in a comforting and enjoyable practice of mindfulness and self-care.

Follow these instructions to set up and test your own ritual:

1. Think of something you do each day, ideally something quick and easy. Having your morning coffee is a good one, but you could also pick brushing your teeth, greeting your dog at the end of the day, or anything else you do regularly.

2. Make it a ritual. From now on, decide to approach this activity with purpose and intention, staying present and mindful as you do it (see Practice Basic Mindfulness in Chapter 9 to learn how). Use it as a trigger to be more engaged in your own life and to enjoy the little things as they happen.

3. If you can, test out your ritual right away. See if it works to enhance your mindset. If not, go back to the first step and pick another activity.

MEDITATE TO FIND
YOUR BALANCE

To be more compassionate and caring for yourself, it's important to find the right balance of work, fun, relationships, hobbies, and relaxation. This balance differs for everyone, but there is a good general rule to follow: Your life should never be more than half of any of these things (e.g., not 60 percent work, or 80 percent fun, or 50 percent relationships). These percentages don't measure how much effort or care you put into these aspects of your life; it's more of a measure of your time and energy. To live a happy, healthy life, it's vital to find your balance between these five domains. Try this meditation to figure out where that balance is.

1. Keeping your eyes closed, think about how much time you put into work, fun, relationships, hobbies, and relaxation. You don't need a precise number; your best estimate is fine.

2. Consider these estimates. Are you happy with how much time and energy you put into each domain? Do you feel any area is being neglected?

3. Think about what the right mix for you would be. How much of your life should be taken up by work? How much by fun? How much by building and maintaining your relationships? Imagine your perfect schedule—for your entire day, not just work—and imagine what it would look like.

4. If you're far off from your ideal schedule, commit to working on moving toward your balance. Thank yourself for taking the time to meditate, and go forth to take that commitment and turn it into action!

LET GO OF WHAT YOU DON'T NEED

Do you ever find thoughts floating around your head that you just don't need? Don't worry; we all do sometimes. Even the most positive person occasionally experiences some self-doubt, shame, unnecessary anger, or other negative thoughts from time to time; it's perfectly normal. But if you want to boost your self-compassion and be caring toward yourself, it's good to practice letting go.

1. Take in a deep breath, hold it for two seconds, then let it all out in a big sigh.
2. Think about the negative thoughts you're dealing with right now. Identify them and put a label on them (e.g., "anger," "guilt," or "self-criticism").
3. Gather up all of these thoughts into a word cloud in your mind. See the dark, stormy cloud teeming with the negative thoughts.
4. Now take another big, deep breath in and pause for a moment. When you exhale, make it a big, loud sigh out of your mouth. As you breathe, watch the cloud; see it quiver as you draw your breath in, then watch it float away as you exhale.
5. Take another deep breath and exhale, pushing the cloud even farther away. Continue until the cloud is completely gone, then continue your day with a fresh mind free from negative thoughts.

INHALE THE GOOD, EXHALE THE BAD

This meditation will help you take in what is around you without taking in all the negative or unhealthy stuff along with the good. It's great to be open and receptive, but you also need to be careful about what you consume—not only the food and drink you consume but the thoughts, words, images, and so on. To make sure you're avoiding the bad stuff while not missing out on the good stuff, practice the following meditation.

1. When you're ready to begin, turn your attention back to your breath. Get to a steady pace, breathing in and out slowly.
2. Now imagine that all the good things around you—the love, joy, pleasure, all things positive and pleasant—can be inhaled into you. All you need to do is take a big breath in, and you will bring all of this goodness in with your breath.
3. Imagine that, not only can you inhale all the good, you can exhale all the bad. Everything negative or sad or angry inside of you can be driven away simply by exhaling sharply.
4. Practice it. Visualize all the good things around you entering your body as you take in a breath of air. Hold it for a moment and allow the good things to settle in, then watch as all the negativity rushes out as you exhale. Continue for a few breaths until you feel nothing but good energy.

GIVE YOURSELF A BREAK

When was the last time you gave yourself a break—not a time break, but a compassion break? If you're currently experiencing a rough moment and you've never given yourself a self-compassion break before, there's no time like the present to give it a try! The following steps explain how to engage in a quick, simple self-compassion meditation.

1. Come into your practice with an open mind, but don't try to force out the negative feelings. Sit with them, and allow yourself to feel them.
2. Say to yourself, "This sucks. It hurts, and I don't like it." Repeat it a couple of times until you feel like you've accepted your current struggle.
3. Now say to yourself, "But that's life. Sometimes I struggle and that's okay." Again, repeat it as many times as you need to in order to feel a sense of peace.
4. Finally, say, "I will be kind to myself. I will be patient with myself. I will be compassionate toward myself." Continue until you feel the spark of self-compassion.
5. Tell yourself that life is hard sometimes, but you are always here for yourself. You deserve to take a self-compassion break whenever you need one, and you *can* take one whenever you need one.

INDEX

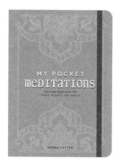
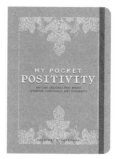

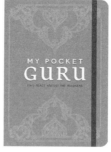